Little Tables

Anytime Breakfasts
from around the World

Beatnik

First published in 2016 by Beatnik Publishing

Copyright © Beatnik Publishing 2016
Photographer: © Vanessa Lewis
Designer: © Elena van Renen & © Beatnik Design
Hair Stylist: Alek Daray
Fashion Stylist: Jodie Ennik
Food Stylist: Taryne Jakobi
Writer: © Amy Searll

Printed and bound in China.

ISBN 978-0-9941205-9-5

Beatnik Publishing

PO Box 8276, Symonds Street,
Auckland 1150, New Zealand

www.beatnikpublishing.com

Little Tables

Anytime Breakfasts
from around the World

VANESSA LEWIS

Dedicated to Nina,
who would eat cake before anything,
with the same passion she has for life

FOREWORD

Whoever we are and wherever we come from, we all mark significant cultural and emotional moments with food. There is identity in each sip of soup and every biscuit crumb. Where I'm from, we associate "Japaneseness" with every mouthful of sushi and Easter with a bite of hot cross bun.

Vanessa Lewis has captured such moments with a quiet, understated elegance. She has a personal humility and stillness that has elicited a calm confidence in her photographic subjects. Her kind, patient manner has been rewarded with authenticity in every gaze. Each portrait not only reflects the unique essence of the individual child but also a charming bite-sized morsel of culinary culture. Her images are sweet but never cloying. Her recipes are representative but never clichéd.

Anna Trapido ~ Food writer, Broadcaster, Author,
Food Culture Enthusiast, Mum to Josiah

A Note from the Author

I grew up on around seven different breakfast offerings which coincided with the days of the week, depending on my mood and my mum's conviction for the day. Rice Krispies (popped rice cereal) were a favourite and "French toast" (fried egg-dipped bread) was a weekend treat. My grandmother used to make the best maize porridge topped with fried minced meat for my sleepover breakfast at her house. To this day, I cherish the memory of that taste – a childhood experience embedded in a unique culture of breakfast.

This book investigates and celebrates breakfast dishes, not only as morning meals, but also as comfort food and indulgences for any time of the day. Of course, one culture's soul food is another's exciting culinary adventure. Taking us from Jamaica to Jordan, Canada to China, these recipes are inspired by national food cultures and are not necessarily each country's most popular meal. Rather, they have been chosen to create a varied recipe book: baked goods; eggy dishes; fish; rice and noodle bowls; five-minute breakfasts and weekend indulgences.

I love to photograph food and children, particularly my daughter Nina. For this project, I created little sets to represent kitchens or dining rooms using the same table angle, so the table becomes one long table running through the book – or through the world for that matter. It was challenging to tell three and four-year olds they had to wear unfamiliar clothing, not eat the food placed in front of them and not play with the carefully-placed toys on the table! However, it was most rewarding when they tried the "new" food after the shoot and loved it, looking at their mums and dads and asking if they could make it at home. Every child brought their own magic to the shoot, and they were all true superstars in my world.

I hope, through *Little Tables*, you enjoy encountering new flavours and rediscovering childhood favourites.

Vanessa Lewis

CONTENTS

Australia

Contrary to popular belief, rolled-oat biscuits were not sent to soldiers on the Front, but were instead sold at fundraising events for the war effort. And these "soldiers' biscuits" weren't referred to as "Anzac" biscuits in a cookbook until 1921.

Anzac Biscuits
Vegetarian

Makes 12 medium biscuits

INGREDIENTS

320g (11.3oz) rolled oats
250g (8.8oz) flour
150g (5.3oz) desiccated coconut
100g (3.5oz) sugar
250g (8.8 oz) butter
60ml golden syrup
1 tsp baking soda
2 Tbsp boiling water

To Serve
glass of milk
or cup of tea for dunking biscuits

METHOD

Preheat the oven to 160°C. Lightly grease 2 baking sheets. Put the oats, flour, coconut and sugar into a big mixing bowl. In a medium saucepan, melt the butter and golden syrup over low heat. As soon as the butter has melted, take the saucepan off the heat. Meanwhile, mix the baking soda and boiling water in a cup. Add this to the melted butter mixture in the saucepan, then quickly add the butter and baking soda mixture to the oat and flour mixture. Mix well. Take tablespoons of the mixture and roll into balls. Place the biscuit balls on the baking sheets 5cm apart. Press down lightly with a fork to flatten. Bake for 15 - 20 minutes.

Aa
Australia

Dippy Eggs
& Vegemite Soldiers
Vegetarian

Serves 4

INGREDIENTS

4 extra large **eggs**
4 slices **wholewheat** or **Low GI bread**
butter for spreading
Vegemite or **Marmite**

Optional
cheddar cheese, sliced

METHOD

Place eggs in a saucepan and add enough cold water to cover them by about 2cm. Place the pan over medium-high heat and as soon as the water reaches a brisk simmer, start timing. As the eggs cook, adjust the heat as needed to maintain a brisk simmer, rather than a rapid boil. For soft-boiled eggs, cook for 2 ½ minutes. For medium-boiled eggs, cook for 4 ½ minutes (for hard-boiled eggs, it would be 8 minutes, but you don't want hard yolks for Dippy Eggs).

Meanwhile, toast the bread. Spread on some butter and Vegemite. Cut the toast into fingers. When the eggs are done, slice the top off the eggs. Season with salt and pepper. Serve with toast "soldiers" and dip away!

Optional
Top the Vegemite toast with cheese and place under a hot grill for 2 - 3 minutes. Slice and dip into your eggs.

Cc
Canada

Over eighty percent of the world's maple syrup comes from Canada. December 17th is their National Maple Syrup Day. The sweet, dark and luscious liquid gold is delicious in both sweet and savoury dishes and eaten anytime from morning till night.

Cinnamon Buns
Vegetarian

Makes 18 buns

INGREDIENTS

Dough
250ml full cream milk
3 Tbsp butter
440g (15.4oz) flour
100g (3.5oz) sugar
1 large egg
2 tsp instant dried yeast
1 tsp salt

Filling
150g (5.3oz) brown sugar
2 Tbsp ground cinnamon
60g (2oz) butter, softened

Icing
120g (4oz) cream cheese, at room temperature
130g (4.6oz) icing sugar
60g (2oz) butter, softened
½ tsp vanilla extract

METHOD

Dough
Gently heat the milk and butter together until the mixture is just warm and the butter has melted. Pour this into the bowl of a free-standing electric mixer that's been fitted with a paddle attachment. Add a quarter of the flour and the sugar, egg, yeast and salt. Beat on a low speed for 3 minutes. Add the rest of the flour and beat on a low speed until all of the flour is incorporated and the dough is quite sticky. Add a little more flour if needed.

Turn the dough out onto a lightly-floured work surface and knead until smooth and elastic. Form into a ball and place in a lightly-oiled bowl covered in plastic wrap. Leave to rise in a warm place for about 2 hours, or until it has doubled in size. Knock back the dough and return it to the floured work surface. Roll it into a 40 x 25cm rectangle.

Filling
Spread the butter over the dough, leaving a 1cm border. Combine the cinnamon and sugar and sprinkle evenly over the butter. Starting at one long side, roll the dough into a log. With the seam-side down, cut the dough crosswise into 18 equal slices.

Grease 2 baking trays and divide the rolls between them, covering with plastic wrap. Allow to rise in a warm place until the buns have doubled in size – about 40 minutes. Preheat the oven to 190°C. Bake the buns on the middle shelf for 20 - 25 minutes, or until the tops are golden. Remove from the tray and allow to cool.

Icing
Combine the cream cheese, icing sugar, butter and vanilla in a mixing bowl and beat with an electric mixer until smooth. Spread the icing on top of the cooled rolls. Serve warm or at room temperature.

Cc
Canada

Fèves au Lard
Maple Baked Beans ~ Gluten-free

Serves 10 – 12 as a side dish

INGREDIENTS

450g (15.9oz) **dried navy (haricot) beans***, soaked overnight and drained.
230g (8.1oz) **pork belly,** roughly chopped
1 **onion**, finely chopped
1½ tsp **salt**
1 tsp **milled black pepper**
500 - 750ml **real maple syrup**
2 tsp **Dijon mustard**
1.5L **water**

To Serve
crusty bread (gluten-free if required)

*Though it's not as authentic, if you can't find navy beans, you can also use cannellini, kidney, or black beans.

If you're cooking this for just one or two people, halve the recipe and you should have no trouble finishing it in a couple days – at most.

METHOD

Preheat the oven to 180°C. In a large casserole dish, stir together the beans, pork belly, onion, salt, pepper, syrup, and mustard. Add the water and bring to the boil on the element. Cover the dish and bake for 1 hour 30 minutes, stirring occasionally. Uncover and bake for an additional 60 - 70 minutes or until the beans have absorbed most of the liquid and the top is browned and crusty.

Serve at once with soft, white bread or crusty bread rolls.

> *Cook's Note –* This makes a wonderful bush or campsite breakfast. Serve in bowls with toasted corn bread as a delicious accompaniment.

Cc
China

Food is such an important part of Chinese culture that it even comes up in greetings. When two Chinese people bump into each other, they will often say, "Have you eaten yet?" instead of, "Hello, how are you?"

Dim Sum
Pork and Ginger Wontons with Spicy Plum Dipping Sauce

Makes 20

INGREDIENTS

250g (8.8oz) **pork mince**
5cm piece **fresh ginger,**
peeled and finely grated
2 cloves **garlic,** crushed
1 Tbsp **soy sauce**
1 Tbsp **Chinese rice wine**
1 Tbsp **fresh chives,** finely chopped
1 small **baby cabbage,** finely shredded
20 gow gee pastry **wonton wrappers***

Spicy Plum Dipping Sauce
80ml **plum sauce**
3 Tbsp **sweet chilli sauce**
½ tsp **ground Chinese five spice**
1 tsp **lime juice**

*Wonton wrappers are available in the freezer aisle in Asian supermarkets, in squares or rounds.

METHOD

Place all the ingredients, excluding the wonton wrappers, into a bowl and mix together thoroughly. Spoon 1 heaped teaspoonful of the mixture into the center of each wrapper. Brush the edge of the wonton wrapper with cold water and fold the wrappers over to enclose filling. Pleat edges together to seal. Place dumplings on a tray lined with baking paper. Place a large bamboo steamer lined with baking paper over a wok or large saucepan of simmering water. Steam the dumplings, covered, in batches, for 5 - 6 minutes, or until cooked through. Meanwhile, combine the spicy plum dipping sauce ingredients in a small bowl. Transfer dumplings to a plate. Serve at once with the plum sauce or soy sauce.

Cc
China

Congee
Rice Porridge ~ Gluten-free

Serves 4 – 6

INGREDIENTS

1.5L water
945ml good-quality **chicken stock**
3 **skinless bone-in chicken legs** or **thighs**
210g (7.4oz) **long grain white rice**
3cm unpeeled piece **ginger**,
sliced into 4 pieces
2 tsp **salt**, plus more to taste
½ tsp **white pepper**

To Garnish

sesame oil
fresh coriander, roughly chopped
spring onion, thinly sliced
Chinese dried sausage, sliced
red or green chilli, thinly sliced

Congee is a soft, savoury Chinese porridge made from rice. This version with shredded chicken and fresh ginger is simple to make and very tasty indeed.

METHOD

Put all the ingredients in a large, heavy-bottomed saucepan. Bring to the boil over medium-high heat. Once boiling, reduce the heat and cook at a lively simmer, stirring occasionally until the rice is soft and the mixture is creamy – about 1 hour.

Then turn off the heat and remove the chicken with a slotted spoon. When it's cool enough to handle, shred into bite-sized pieces, discarding the bones. Place the shredded chicken back in the saucepan, stir to combine and add salt to taste. Ladle into deep bowls, drizzle with a few drops of sesame oil and top with any or all of the garnishes.

Cc
Cuba

When the clock strikes midnight on New Year's Eve in Cuba, it means it's time to eat grapes. It's an old Cuban tradition imported from Spain; everyone eats twelve grapes and makes twelve wishes for the upcoming year.

Arroz con Leche
Rice Pudding ~ Vegetarian, Gluten-free

Serves 4

INGREDIENTS

210g (7.4oz) long grain rice
2 cinnamon sticks
2 strips of lemon or orange rind
3 whole cloves or ½ tsp ground cloves
1L water
1 egg
750ml full cream milk
340g (12oz) tin sweetened
condensed milk
½ tsp salt
1 Tbsp vanilla extract
75g (2.6oz) raisins or sultanas (optional)

To Serve (optional)
cream, to pour
bananas, sliced

Similar to English rice pudding, this dish is flavoured with cinnamon and citrus rind but is traditionally served cold instead of hot.

METHOD

Put the rice, cinnamon sticks, lemon or orange rind and cloves into a heavy-bottomed saucepan. Add the water and soak for 1 hour. Then put the saucepan on the stove and bring the rice mixture to the boil on high heat. Once it's boiling, lower the heat and cook the rice for 10 - 15 minutes or until the water has almost evaporated. While the rice is cooking, beat the egg, then add the milk to it. Pour the egg and milk mixture, condensed milk, salt, vanilla extract and raisins or sultanas in with the rice. Cook over medium heat, stirring constantly until the mixture thickens and the rice has absorbed most of the liquid. This should take about 20 - 30 minutes, but watch carefully because it might cook faster. If you like a thinner pudding, take the rice off the heat before the mixture has thickened. Remove the citrus rind and cinnamon sticks and allow to cool uncovered, then chill in the fridge before serving.

Cc
Cuba

Black Bean Oatmeal
Gluten-free

Serves 4

INGREDIENTS

90g (3.2oz) **steel-cut oats** (gluten-free if required)

750ml **water**

2 Tbsp **olive oil**

2 pieces of firm, ripe **plantain** or **sweet potato,** chopped

1 large **onion**, diced

1 **yellow pepper**, diced

125ml good-quality **chicken stock** (gluten-free if required)

425g (14.9oz) tin **black beans**, rinsed and drained

1 tsp **ground cumin**

salt and **pepper**, to taste

To Serve
fresh coriander

Steel-cut oats – also known as coarse oatmeal, or Irish or Scottish oats – are coarsely chopped, as opposed to rolled oats which are steamed and rolled. They look like chopped rice, take longer to cook than rolled oats and retain a chewy consistency.

METHOD

Boil the water and add the oats. Reduce heat to low then cover and cook for 15 - 20 minutes, stirring occasionally. Remove from heat and set aside. Pour 1 tablespoon of the olive oil into a medium, heavy-bottomed frying pan and warm over medium heat. Add the plantains and cook for 4 - 5 minutes – or, if you're using sweet potatoes, 20 - 25 minutes – until they're golden brown. Turn them occasionally so they don't stick to the pan. Remove from the pan and set aside. Heat the rest of the olive oil in the pan and fry the onion and yellow pepper until the onion is translucent and the pepper is soft. Add the beans, chicken stock, cumin, salt and pepper to the pan and cook for 20 - 25 minutes, or until the beans are piping hot. Divide the oatmeal into bowls and spoon the bean mixture over it. Serve with fresh coriander.

Denmark

Denmark is reported to be the happiest country in the world. The Danes definitely have a sense of humour; there is a Danish candy-making company called BonBon that's famous for giving its treats odd names. The sweets they make are called things like "Burping Duck"and "Seagull Droppings". Luckily, their traditional morning bites sound a lot more appealing.

Salmon Smørrebrød

Smørrebrød roughly translates to "butter and bread". They are traditional Danish open sandwiches made with dark rye bread. Generally, these sandwiches – each with different toppings such as cold meat, smoked fish and cheese – will be served all together as a meal and each will be served with, and decorated by, visually-appealing accompaniments.

*Serves 2 – 4
depending on appetite*

INGREDIENTS

3 Tbsp **crème fraiche** or **sour cream**
4 slices **Danish rye bread**, cut into circles
250g (8.8oz) **smoked salmon** or **salmon trout slices**
3 **radishes**, thinly sliced
2 Tbsp **salmon** or **salmon trout roe** (optional)
salt and **milled black pepper**

To Serve
dill sprigs and flat-leaf parsley
lemon wedges

METHOD

Spread the crème fraiche or sour cream onto the Danish rye, then top with smoked salmon, sliced radish, salmon or salmon trout roe. Sprinkle over the dill and parsley.

Season with salt and pepper.

> *Cook's Note* – Other Smørrebrød ideas:
> hard-boiled eggs, prawns and mayonnaise
> smoked eel, scrambled eggs, sliced radishes and chopped chives
> liver pâté with crispy bacon and sautéed mushrooms
> pickled cucumber, hard-boiled eggs and red onion
> roast beef, remoulade, horseradish and crispy fried onion.

Dd
Denmark

Makes enough to scatter over 4 – 6 bowls of yoghurt

INGREDIENTS

200g (7oz) **dark Danish rye bread**
2 Tbsp **dark brown sugar**
1 tsp **mixed spice** (optional)

To Serve (optional – whichever combination you like)
thick Greek-style yoghurt
honey
seasonal red berries
chopped dried figs, crystallized ginger
and finely grated orange zest
goji berries, dried cranberries
and poppy seeds

Ymerdrys
Vegetarian

Ymerdrys is a crunchy, sweet topping, made with the crumbs of leftover or stale authentic, heavy, waxy and dense Danish rye bread. The crispy, malty mixture is served with fresh berries and Ymer, a Danish version of sour milk. But a luscious, double-thick yoghurt is our favourite.

METHOD

Preheat the oven to 190°C. Break the bread into large chunks and place into the bowl of a food processor. Add the sugar and spice (if using), and pulse until a crumbly mixture forms.

Spread the crumble in an even layer onto a baking tray lined with baking paper. Bake for 10 - 15 minutes until crispy. Watch it closely for the last 5 minutes of cooking to make sure the mixture doesn't burn. Cool completely on the baking tray before serving. Serve sprinkled over yoghurt and berries, or your preferred topping.

Ee
Egypt

If you are invited to an Egyptian home, you should take small gifts of food like chocolates, pastries or sweets. Don't take flowers – this is seen as bad luck in Egypt because flowers are usually reserved for weddings.

Tahini & Molasses
Vegetarian

Serves 1

INGREDIENTS

3 Tbsp **tahini**
3 Tbsp **molasses**
1 **lemon wedge**
1 **pita bread**, toasted if desired

METHOD

Pour the tahini into a serving bowl. Drizzle over the molasses and squeeze the lemon juice over the top. Mix just a little. Dip pita wedges into the mixture.

Cook's Note – You can also serve fresh figs, dates and sliced apples with the mixture.

Ee
Egypt

Shakshouka

Vegetarian, Gluten-free

Serves 4

INGREDIENTS

1 Tbsp **olive oil**

1 **onion**, diced

1 **green pepper**, diced

2 cloves **garlic**, crushed

400g tin (14.1oz) **whole peeled plum tomatoes with juice**

1 tsp **paprika**

¼ tsp **milled black pepper**

½ tsp **cumin seeds**

4 **eggs**

To Serve

hot buttered toast or pita bread (gluten-free if required)

salt to taste (optional)

Shakshouka is a popular Middle Eastern dish of eggs that have been cooked in a tomato and pepper sauce.

METHOD

In a deep frying pan, heat the oil on medium heat and then sauté the onion, green pepper and garlic until the onion starts to become translucent. Add the tomatoes, paprika, pepper and cumin seeds. Crush the tomatoes with a fork or with the back of a spoon. Let the tomato mixture simmer uncovered for about 15 - 20 minutes. Crack the eggs on top of the tomato sauce and cook until they're done to your liking.

Ee
England

Even though she's royalty, the Queen of England loves simple food. For breakfast every morning, she eats cereal with dried fruit and nuts, or toast and marmalade. She also always drinks tea with breakfast.

Roasted Rhubarb Compote & Fry Up
Gluten-free

Pretty-in-pink rhubarb is extremely popular in the British Isles. Too tart and bitter to be eaten raw, it's always served cooked. Serve this delicate compote warm with thick custard. Or, serve it at room temperature with thick, Greek-style yoghurt, pistachio ice cream or an interesting milk-flavoured sorbet.

METHOD

Roasted Rhubarb Compote
Preheat the oven to 190°C. Toss all the ingredients together and arrange in a baking dish. Bake for 25 - 30 minutes, stirring occasionally, until the rhubarb is tender and the juices have become thick and syrupy. Let the rhubarb cool and serve lukewarm or at room temperature.

Cook's Note – Rhubarb has a natural affinity with strawberries and raspberries. Combine and use as a filling for a fruit crumble or tart.

Fry Up
There isn't really a recipe for a traditional fry up, but depending on what part of the country you're in, it can include pork sausages, crispy bacon, kippers, fried potatoes or hash browns, sautéed mushrooms, grilled tomatoes, fried eggs, black pudding and the all-time favourite – baked beans.

We used herbed pork sausages, sautéed mushrooms, grilled tomato and fried eggs for our fry up, but the more the merrier we say. Oh, and don't forget to add a dash of HP Sauce and a slice of lightly-toasted white bread, and wash it all down with a strong cuppa.

Serves 6

INGREDIENTS

Compote
230g (8.1oz) **rhubarb**, sliced into 2cm pieces
75g (2.6oz) **sugar**
3 Tbsp **orange juice**
1 tsp **orange zest**, finely grated
½ tsp **ground ginger**
pinch of **ground cinnamon**

Ee
England

Serves 4 – 6
depending on size of appetite

INGREDIENTS

250g (8.8oz) **long grain white rice**
½ tsp **turmeric** (optional for
saffron-hued rice)
500g (17.6oz) **hot smoked haddock** or
salmon (we used salmon), filleted
1 **lemon**, quartered
3 Tbsp **butter**
1 **onion**, diced
1 Tbsp **medium curry powder**
salt and **milled black pepper**
4 hard-boiled **eggs**, sliced or quartered
1⅓ Tbsp **fresh chives**, cut with scissors
1⅓ Tbsp **fresh dill**, roughly chopped

To Serve
lemon or lime wedges
mango atchar (not entirely traditional,
but a great spicy Afro-Indian addition)

Kedgeree
Gluten-free

METHOD

Combine rice, water, turmeric, and salt in a medium saucepan. Bring to the boil, stir, cover and reduce heat to low. Simmer for 18 - 20 minutes, remove from heat and set aside. Poach the fish by placing the fish fillets and lemon quarters into a large pan. Pour enough water over the top, just barely covering the fish. Place a lid on the pan and bring to the boil. Turn off the heat and allow the fish to poach in the cooking liquid for 10 - 15 minutes, or until the fish is just cooked and flakes easily. Remove the fish from the liquid and break into bite-sized flakes. Melt the butter in a wide pan and fry the onion over low heat for 4 - 5 minutes. Add the curry powder and cook for 1 minute. Carefully stir in the cooked rice and salmon, and heat through. Season well with salt and pepper. Add the eggs and cook for 1 minute. Stir in the chives and dill and serve at once.

Cook's Note – For a more substantial dish, any of the following would make great (and colourful) additions: sautéed diced peppers, halved and grilled cherry tomatoes or chargrilled sweetcorn kernels.

Need a little more spice? Add 1 tablespoon of black mustard seeds, 1 tablespoon of cumin seeds, 3 crushed cardamom pods and some fresh curry leaves at the melted butter stage, and cook for 1 minute, before adding the onions. Replace the chives and dill with torn fresh coriander leaves.

Ff
France

If you peer into the kitchen window of a French bakery, you'll notice that each baguette coming out of the oven is exactly the same. This is because the French Government has very strict rules for making baguettes. Each loaf must weigh exactly 250 grams and measure 50 - 55cm in length.

Cheats' Mini Butter Croissants
Vegetarian

Makes 12 croissants

INGREDIENTS

3 sheets **frozen puff pastry**, defrosted
100g (3.5oz) **unsalted butter**, cut into cubes
1 **egg** and 1 Tbsp **milk** for brushing

To Serve
Brie
French raspberry preserve such as
Bonne Maman
ham or cold cuts
fresh fruit, such as figs, grapes
or strawberries

METHOD

Preheat the oven to 220°C and line 2 baking trays with baking paper. Roll out the dough and cut each sheet of pastry across the diagonals to give you 4 triangles. Dot cubes of butter on top of each triangle. Starting at the base of each triangle, loosely roll it upwards towards the tip. Place the finished croissants on the lined baking trays, curving them into crescent shapes. Brush with egg wash and bake for 15 minutes. Reduce the temperature to 190°C and bake for another 4 - 5 minutes, until they are evenly golden brown. Leave them on the tray to cook internally for another 10 minutes.

Serve warm or at room temperature with preserves, cheeses and cold cuts.

Ff
France

Makes 3 sandwiches

INGREDIENTS

1 Tbsp **Dijon mustard**
2 Tbsp **mayonnaise**
60g (2oz) **butter**, softened
6 slices **white bread**
6 thin slices **Camembert cheese**
12 pieces thinly-sliced **ham**
60g (2oz) **flour**
½ tsp **baking powder**
pinch of **salt**
2 **eggs**
60ml **water**
1 Tbsp **oil**

Simplified Croque Monsieur

The Croque Monsieur is the ultimate fried ham and cheese sandwich.

METHOD

Divide 2 tablespoons of the butter between the 6 slices of bread, spreading a little on each slice. On 3 of the slices, spread a layer of Dijon mustard over the butter and top each slice with 4 slices of ham. Spread a layer of mayonnaise onto the other 3 slices and top each one with 2 slices of cheese. Press the ham and cheese sides of the sandwiches together. Whisk the flour, baking powder, salt, eggs and water until blended in a wide, flat dish. Heat the remaining butter and oil in a large heavy-bottomed pan over medium heat. Dip both sides of each sandwich in the egg mixture and fry in the oil and butter for 3 - 4 minutes per side until golden, crispy and browned, flipping occasionally.

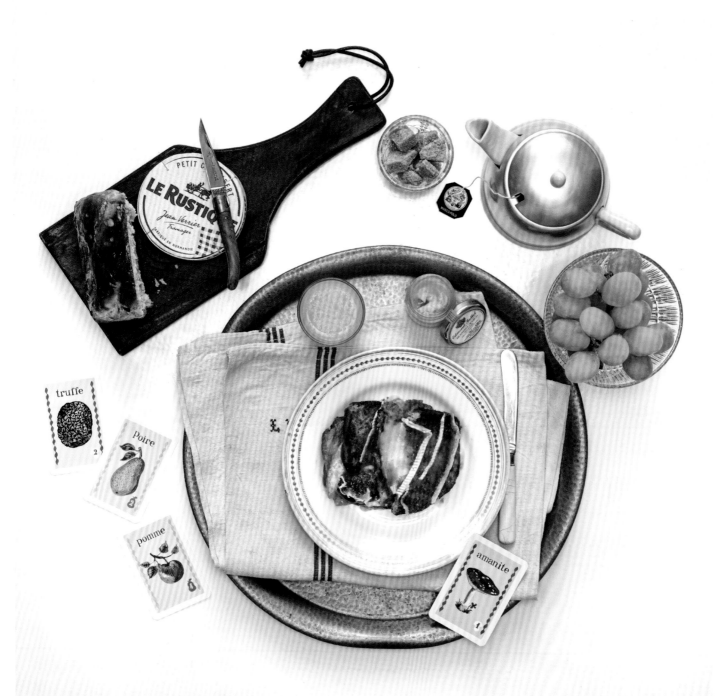

Gg
Greece

In the olive orchards of Greece, you'll find some of the oldest trees in the world. These trees have been around since the thirteenth century and, surprisingly, most of them are still actually producing olives.

Yoghurt, Fruit & Almond Parfait
Vegetarian

Makes 4 starter servings

INGREDIENTS

a handful of **shortbread-style almond biscuits** or **coconut macaroons**, roughly chopped (about 120g/4.2oz)
500g (17.6oz) **Greek-style yoghurt**
250g (8.8oz) **fresh fruit***, chopped
4 Tbsp **flaked almonds**
3 Tbsp **honey**

METHOD

Spoon 2 tablespoons of the yoghurt into the base of each serving glass, then top with a little of the crushed biscuits and a layer of fruit. Add more yoghurt, more crushed biscuits and fruit, repeating the layers until the glass is almost full. Top with the remaining yoghurt, sprinkle over the last of the biscuits and flaked almonds, and top with the remaining fruit. Drizzle with honey and serve at once.

*We used berries, pomegranate rubies and preserved green figs.

Gg
Greece

Froutalia

Makes 1 large froutalia

INGREDIENTS

2 **country-style (pork breakfast) sausages**, cooked and sliced
3 **potatoes**, cooked, peeled and thinly sliced
100g (3.5oz) **pitted green olives**, halved
6 - 8 large **eggs**
125ml **full cream milk**
100g (3.5oz) **cheddar cheese**, grated
3 Tbsp **fresh mint**, chopped
3 Tbsp **flat-leaf parsley**, chopped
salt and **milled black pepper**, to taste
oil for frying

To Serve
crusty bread
Xoriatiki (Greek feta cheese) salad

Froutalia is the Greek version of a frittata or baked omelette. Unlike a Spanish frittata that is usually filled with potato and onion, a Greek froutalia is traditionally filled with sausage, potato and cheese.

METHOD

Preheat the oven to 180°C. Grease a large, heavy-bottomed non-stick pan (that can go in the oven) with enough oil to cover the bottom, then warm over medium heat. Add the sausages and fry for about 4 minutes until the sausages are crispy and browned on both sides. Remove from the pan and drain them on a paper towel. Put a little more oil in the pan, add the sliced potatoes and fry until softened – about 7 - 8 minutes. Then tilt the pan and pour out the extra oil; return the sausages back into the pan with the potatoes and add the olives. In a large bowl, beat the eggs and milk until well combined, then add the cheese, herbs, salt and pepper.

Pour the egg mixture over the sausages and potatoes, cover with a lid bigger than the pan and cook the froutalia over a medium heat for 15 - 20 minutes, depending on the depth of the pan. Brown the top in the preheated oven for 5 - 7 minutes, until golden and brown.

Serve with some crusty bread and a Xoriatiki (Greek feta cheese) salad.

Iceland

In Iceland, they are so mad about herrings that there's a museum in Siglufjordur dedicated just to them. Herrings, along with other fish and seafood, are eaten all year round, and are suitable at any time of the day and for any occasion.

Yoghurt Bark
Vegetarian

Serves 3 – 4

INGREDIENTS

50g (1.8oz) **desiccated coconut**
500g (17.6oz) **thick plain yoghurt**, strained
1 **vanilla pod**, seeds only
120g (4.2oz) **roasted granola**
125g (4.4oz) **fresh berries** such as blueberries, raspberries and blackberries

To Serve
honey or golden syrup

METHOD

Dry fry the coconut in a hot pan over medium heat for 1 - 2 minutes or until lightly golden and crispy. Transfer to a plate and allow to cool. Line a square glass Pyrex dish with wax paper. Mix the yoghurt and vanilla together and pour half of the mixture into the base of the pan. Top with half of the berries and sprinkle half the granola over the berries. Layer the remaining yoghurt and granola and sprinkle the toasted coconut and berries on top. Freeze overnight. Before serving, transfer the dish to the fridge for 10 - 15 minutes to soften slightly. Invert the dish onto a chopping board and remove the yoghurt bark from the dish. Use a large, sharp knife to cut the bark into rough pieces or wedges. Serve at once with honey or golden syrup, if desired.

Ii
Iceland

Herrings on Toast

Makes 6 rollmops or pieces of herring

INGREDIENTS

3 salted herrings
200ml white vinegar
200ml water
80g (2.8oz) sugar
1 onion
6 black peppercorns

To Serve
dark bread such as rye, toasted
cream cheese
gherkins and pickled vegetables

METHOD

First, desalt the herrings: wash them under cold, running water and soak in plenty of cold water for 24 hours, changing the water regularly. Fillet the fish and soak in cold water for another 1 - 2 hours. Cut each fish fillet diagonally across into finger-sized pieces or roll the fillets up starting from the tail, then place into a sterilised jar. Combine the vinegar, water, sugar, onion and peppercorns, and pour this over the herring until covered. Seal the jar and leave in the fridge for a few days to marinate. Serve with hot buttered toast, cream cheese and pickled vegetables, if desired.

India

In 2009, the people of Bhanvad, Jamnagar in India reported that it was raining fish. It's likely that a strong whirlwind swept the fish out of the river and into the air, making it rain fish all over the town.

Yellow Dhal with Banana, Lime & Coconut Lassi

Vegetarian, Gluten-free

Serves 3

INGREDIENTS

Dhal

200g (7oz) dry yellow split peas
2 Tbsp butter
2 tsp oil
1 small onion, chopped
2 cloves garlic, crushed
1 tsp fresh ginger, finely grated
500ml vegetable stock (gluten-free if required)
125ml - 250ml water
pinch of salt
1 Tbsp mild or medium curry powder
1 Tbsp ground cumin
1 tsp ground coriander
pinch of turmeric
¾ tsp garam masala (optional)
10 fresh curry leaves

Lassi

250g (8.8oz) Greek-style yoghurt
2 bananas, peeled
125ml coconut milk, chilled
4 ice cubes
1 tsp honey
4 whole cardamom pods
1 tsp lime zest, finely grated

METHOD

Yellow Dhal

In a medium saucepan, melt the butter over medium heat. Add the oil, onion and salt and fry for 4 - 5 minutes or until the onion has softened. Add the garlic and fry gently for 30 seconds until fragrant. Add the remaining spices and curry leaves and stir well, cooking for 1 minute. Add the split peas and mix well to coat. Stir in the stock and 125ml water, then bring to the boil. Cover and reduce the heat.

Simmer for 40 - 50 minutes or until peas are tender and most of the liquid has been absorbed. You may need to add more water during cooking if the split peas are absorbing the liquid too quickly. Finally, stir in the garam masala and garnish with fresh coriander before serving.

Banana, Lime and Coconut Lassi

A lassi is a popular, yoghurt-based drink from the Punjab region of India. Spices, mint and salt are added to make a savoury salty lassi, while fruit and honey can be added to make a sweet lassi.

Place all the ingredients into a blender and blitz until smooth. Pour the lassi through a sieve to extract the cardamom husks and lime zest. Pour into chilled glasses and serve at once.

Ii
India

Serves 4

INGREDIENTS

315g (11.1oz) **basmati rice**
¾ tsp **turmeric**
1 tsp **sugar**, to taste
¾ tsp **salt**, to taste
2 Tbsp whole **raw peanuts**
2 Tbsp **oil**
1 **potato**, cooked, peeled and cubed
1 tsp **mustard seeds**
1 tsp **cumin seeds**
1 **onion** or **red onion**, finely chopped
10 **curry leaves**

To Serve
desiccated coconut, toasted if desired
coriander leaves
1 lemon, cut into wedges
mango chutney (optional)

Kanda Batata Poha
Vegetarian, Gluten-free

This spiced rice dish is a staple breakfast dish from the Maharashtra state and is made with onions (kanda), potato (batata) and rice. It's a quick, easy and healthy option for breakfast or brunch.

METHOD

Boil the rice until just cooked.

Put the rice in a bowl, then add the turmeric, sugar and salt, and mix to combine. Set aside. Toast the peanuts in a dry pan and set aside. Heat the oil in a medium, heavy-bottomed pan and fry the chopped potato until golden brown, then remove from the pan with a slotted spoon and set aside. Add the mustard seeds to the same pan and fry until they're spluttering. Then add the cumin seeds and cook for another 1 - 2 minutes. Once the cumin seeds are sizzling, add the onions and cook until the onions are transparent and soft. Then add the curry leaves and roasted peanuts and cook for about 1 minute. Put the rice and fried potatoes in the pan and mix gently. Turn the heat to low and cook for about 5 minutes. Garnish with desiccated coconut and coriander leaves and serve with lemon wedges and mango chutney, if desired.

Ireland

The national dish of Ireland is hearty Irish stew made with lamb and potatoes. The Irish are so fond of this stew that they wrote a poem about it.

*"Then hurrah for an Irish stew
That will stick to your belly like glue."*

Boxty Pancakes
Vegetarian

Makes 6 – 8

INGREDIENTS

210g (7.4oz) cooked, **mashed potatoes**
270g (9.5oz) **raw potato**, grated
5 **spring onions**, thinly sliced
2 Tbsp **parsley**, finely chopped
250g (8.8oz) **flour**
1 tsp **baking powder**
1 tsp **kosher** or **sea salt**
½ tsp **ground white pepper**
or **milled black pepper**
240ml **milk**
125g (4.4oz) **Irish cheddar cheese**, grated
1 Tbsp **butter**
1 Tbsp **oil**

To Serve
chives, chopped
sour cream (optional)
smoked salmon slices (optional)

METHOD

Combine the mashed potatoes, grated potato, spring onion and parsley in a large mixing bowl. Sift the flour, baking powder, salt and pepper over the potato mixture and stir to combine. Gradually add the milk and cheese and stir gently, being careful not to overmix. The mixture should be like a very firm, dough-like batter. Heat a non-stick frying pan over medium-high heat and add a little of the butter and the oil. Once the butter has melted, scoop some of the batter into the pan. Flatten and shape into a nice, round pancake shape and fry for 2 - 3 minutes per side or until golden brown on both sides. Turn the heat down if they are browning too quickly.

Continue to add a little butter and fry the "boxty" until all the batter is finished. Serve hot with chopped chives, sour cream and smoked salmon (non-vegetarian option).

Ireland

Irish Barmbrack Fruit Loaf
Vegetarian

Makes 1 large loaf

INGREDIENTS

500ml **English** or **Ceylon tea**, cooled
115g (4oz) **raisins**
75g (2.6oz) **dried currants**, **dried cranberries** or **dried cherries**
2 Tbsp **glacé lemon**
2 Tbsp **orange peel**, minced
250g (8.8oz) **flour**
50g (1.8oz) **light brown sugar**
2 tsp **baking soda**
1 tsp **ground cinnamon**
pinch of freshly **grated nutmeg**
pinch of **ground cloves**
85g (3oz) **unsalted butter**, plus extra
60ml **full cream milk**
1 **egg**, beaten
assorted charms, wrapped individually in baking paper
80ml **honey**, warmed

To Serve
Irish butter
apple wedges
mature cheddar cheese

Traditionally for Halloween, various objects would be baked into the Barmbrack. If you received a slice containing a pea, it meant you would not marry that year, but a slice hiding a ring suggested you would marry. A hidden stick foretold an unhappy marriage, while a piece of cloth foretold poverty, and a sixpence – a relief! – foretold riches.

METHOD

Stir tea, raisins, currants, glacé lemon and orange peel in a bowl, cover with plastic wrap and let sit for 2 hours, then drain and set aside. Preheat the oven to 160°C. Whisk flour, sugar, baking soda, cinnamon, nutmeg and cloves in a bowl, then make a well in the centre. Mix reserved fruit, butter, milk and egg in a bowl and add to the well. Stir until a wet dough forms. Press dough into a greased 20cm cake tin and push charms into dough. Bake until firm – about 35 - 40 minutes. Brush with honey and bake for another 2 minutes. Let the loaf cool slightly before serving sliced with butter, apple and cheese, if you like.

Israel

Israel is famous for its sweet and juicy peppers. In 2013, the largest pepper in the world was grown in the town of Ein Yahav and weighed in at over half a kilo.

Baba Ganoush & Bourekas
Vegetarian

Serves 3 – 4
Makes 18 bourekas

INGREDIENTS

Baba Ganoush
2 large aubergines
3 Tbsp extra virgin olive oil
3 Tbsp tahini (sesame paste)
3 - 4 cloves garlic, crushed
2 Tbsp lemon juice
1 tsp ground cumin
½ tsp cayenne pepper
salt and milled black pepper

To Serve
1 Tbsp olive oil
1 Tbsp flat-leaf parsley, chopped
warmed and/or toasted pita bread

Bourekas Filling
150g (5.3oz) feta cheese, crumbled
100g (3.5oz) mozzarella cheese, grated
100g (3.5oz) smooth cream cheese
2 egg yolks
1 Tbsp cornflour
milled black pepper

Bourekas Pastry
2 sheets of frozen puff pastry, defrosted
1 egg beaten with 15ml water for brushing
2 Tbsp black or white sesame seeds

Baba ganoush is a luscious Levantine dip made from meltingly-tender roasted aubergine and lashings of garlic. Bourekas are small triangles of flaky dough filled with soft white cheese. Our version has some mozzarella cheese inside, not strictly traditional, but we love the soft, stringy texture it adds to these tasty morsels.

METHOD

Baba Ganoush
Preheat the oven to 200°C. Prick the aubergines in several places with a fork and cut in half lengthwise. Brush the cut sides with 1 tablespoon of olive oil. Place the aubergine halves on a baking tray, cut side down, and roast until very tender – about 35 - 40 minutes. Remove from the oven and allow to cool for 15 minutes.

Scoop the aubergine flesh into a large bowl and mash well with a fork. Add the garlic, the remaining 2 tablespoons of olive oil, tahini, lemon juice, cumin and cayenne pepper. Season to taste with salt and pepper, adding extra lemon juice and cayenne pepper, if required. Mash well until you have a mixture that's smooth but still has some of the aubergine texture.

Allow the baba ganoush to cool to room temperature and swirl a little olive oil over the top. Finish with fresh chopped parsley. Serve with warm pita bread.

Bourekas Filling
Preheat the oven to 180°C and line 2 baking trays with baking paper. Place the cream cheese, egg yolks and cornflour into a mixing bowl and beat until smooth. Stir in the remaining ingredients and mix until well combined.

Bourekas Pastry
Roll out each pastry sheet onto a lightly-floured surface until it's a ½ cm thick, creating a 12 x 12 cm square. Cut the pastry into 9 squares per sheet. Place 1 tablespoon of filling into the centre of each square, fold diagonally to form a triangle and pinch the edges together to seal. Arrange the bourekas with sufficient space between them to rise on the baking sheets. Brush the triangles with the beaten egg mixture and sprinkle the sesame seeds over the top. Bake for 20 - 30 minutes until the bourekas are puffed up and golden.

Israel

Israeli Salad & Hummus

Vegetarian, Gluten-free

Serves 8

INGREDIENTS

Israeli Salad
500g (17.6oz) Lebanese cucumbers*, diced
450g (15.9oz) fresh ripe tomatoes,
seeded and diced
1 small red onion, finely chopped
4 Tbsp fresh parsley, finely chopped
3 Tbsp extra virgin olive oil
3 Tbsp fresh lemon juice
salt and milled black pepper

Hummus
200g (7oz) chickpeas
2 Tbsp lemon juice
½ tsp lemon zest, finely grated
2 cloves garlic, crushed
1 tsp ground cumin
½ tsp salt
100ml tahini (optional)
60ml water
2 Tbsp extra virgin olive oil
1 tsp paprika

To Serve
4 pita breads (gluten-free if required)

In Israel, breakfast isn't usually just one dish. It normally consists of many small dishes and one of them is always an Israeli salad.

METHOD

Israeli Salad
Place all the ingredients in a large mixing bowl and mix until everything is well combined. Season to taste. This salad is best served fresh at room temperature but is also super refreshing when served chilled.

*If you can't find small Lebanese cucumbers, telegraph cucumbers will work equally well.

Hummus
Drain the chickpeas and rinse well under cold, running water. Reserve a few whole chickpeas for serving. Combine the chickpeas, lemon juice, garlic, cumin, salt, tahini and water in a food processor and blend to a creamy purée. Add more lemon juice, garlic, cumin or salt to taste. Turn the hummus out onto a dinner plate and smooth the surface with the back of a spoon. Drizzle with extra virgin olive oil and scatter with the reserved chickpeas. Sprinkle with paprika and serve with pita bread that's been warmed in a moderate oven for 3 minutes and then cut into quarters.

Italy

In Italy, you're allowed to throw food, as long as it's pasta. If an Italian cook is boiling spaghetti, they will sometimes take one strand out of the pot and throw it against the wall to check if it's ready. If the spaghetti sticks to the wall, that means it's cooked.

Individual Frittatas
Gluten-free

Makes 2 frittatas

INGREDIENTS

non-stick cooking spray
4 large **eggs**
60ml **full cream milk**
salt and **milled black pepper**
115g (4oz) **ham**, roughly chopped
(gluten-free if required)
3 Tbsp **Parmesan cheese**, finely grated
1 Tbsp **Italian (flat-leaf) parsley**, chopped

METHOD

Preheat the oven grill. Grease 2 small ovenproof frying pans with non-stick spray. Break the eggs into a large bowl, add the milk, pepper and salt, and whisk very well. Stir the ham, cheese and parsley into the egg mixture. Ladle this mixture into the pans and cook over medium heat until the eggs are set but still wobbly, then put the pans in the oven for a few minutes until the eggs are cooked through.

Italy

Almond Biscotti

Vegetarian

Makes 16 biscotti / biscuits

INGREDIENTS

170g (6oz) **blanched whole almonds**, toasted and roughly chopped
130g (4.6oz) **white sugar**
2 large **eggs**
1 tsp **almond extract**
1 tsp **baking powder**
½ tsp **salt**
220g (7.8oz) **flour**

METHOD

Preheat the oven to 180°C. Using an electric beater, beat the eggs and sugar until thick – about 5 minutes. You'll know the mixture is ready when you raise the beaters and small ribbons of batter are left behind. Beat in the almond extract and set aside. In another bowl, sift the flour, baking powder and salt. Add this to the egg mixture and stir until combined, then fold in the chopped almonds. This will make a dough. Shape the dough into a log about 30cm long and 9cm wide. Bake the log for about 25 minutes or until the dough is firm. Remove from the oven and cool on a rack for about 10 minutes.

Reduce the oven temperature to 165°C. Put the log on a chopping board and cut it into biscotti that are 2cm thick. Put the biscotti on a baking tray and bake for about 10 minutes each side or until each side is golden. Remove from the oven and cool before serving.

Jj
Jamaica

Jamaicans have some great names for their traditional dishes. There's a Jamaican bread called "Festival", a sweet potato dessert called "Blue Drawers" and a fish pâté called "Solomon Gundy".

Coconut Bread & Tropical Smoothie
Vegetarian

Makes 1 loaf
Serves 2 smoothies

INGREDIENTS

Coconut Bread
2 eggs
300ml coconut milk or full cream milk
1 tsp vanilla essence
310g (10.9oz) flour
2 tsp baking powder
2 tsp ground cinnamon
190g (6.7oz) caster sugar
150g (5.3oz) desiccated coconut
75g (2.6oz) butter, melted

To Serve
creamed honey
nut butters

Tropical Smoothie
1 ripe banana
100g (3.5oz) pineapple or mango, peeled and chopped
80ml tropical fruit juice
125ml vanilla yoghurt
3 - 6 ice cubes (optional)

To Serve
1 fresh passionfruit

METHOD

Coconut Bread
Preheat the oven to 190°C. Lightly whisk the eggs, milk and vanilla together.

Mix all the dry ingredients into a separate bowl to combine. Pour the wet ingredients into the dry ingredients and gently combine, being careful not to overmix. Pour into a greased/lined loaf tin and bake until it's golden and cracked on the top – about 55 - 60 minutes or when a skewer inserted into the centre comes out clean.

To Serve
Creamed honey and/or nut butter such as macadamia, pecan or peanut butter.

Tropical Smoothie
Place all the smoothie ingredients into a blender and blend until smooth. Stir in the passionfruit and serve at once.

Jj
Jamaica

Fish in Escovitch Sauce
Gluten-free

Serves 4 – 6

INGREDIENTS

900g - 1kg (approx 2lbs) of firm,
whole linefish, cleaned and gutted
salt and **milled black pepper**
½ **lime**
2 sprigs **thyme** for each whole fish
1 **spring onions** for each whole fish
1 **Habanero chilli** or 1 - 2 **red chillies**,
stems and seeds removed, thinly sliced
2 Tbsp **olive oil**, plus more for greasing
1 **green**, 1 **yellow** and 1 **red pepper**,
deseeded and thinly sliced
1 **onion** or **red onion**, thinly sliced
1 Tbsp **apple cider vinegar**

To Serve
lime or lemon wedges

METHOD

Preheat the oven to 190°C. Season the cavity of each fish with salt and pepper, and squeeze a little lime juice into each. Stuff each cavity with 2 sprigs of thyme, 1 spring onion and some chilli. Cut 3 diagonal slashes into the side of each fish and season each fish with salt and pepper. Put the fish on a baking tray lined with foil and greased with olive oil, and bake until the fish is just cooked through – about 20 - 30 minutes.

While the fish is cooking, make the sauce by heating the oil in a 30cm heavy-bottomed pan. Add the rest of the chilli, sliced peppers and red onion to the pan and cook for about 5 minutes or until the vegetables have softened slightly but still have a nice crunch to them. Remove the pan from heat, stir in the vinegar and season with salt and pepper. Spoon the sauce over the cooked fish.

Jj
Japan

Traditional Japanese-style breakfasts consist of steamed rice, miso soup and various side dishes such as boiled or grilled fish, tamagoyaki (rolled omelette) or rice with raw eggs, tsukemono pickles and nori (dried seaweed).

Ozoni with Mochi
Vegetarian, Gluten-free

This light, fragrant vegetable broth is filled with small mochi – little glutinous rice flour cakes. You can make the bite-sized mochi any shape you like. Ozoni is served in the morning on New Year's Day in households throughout Japan, with each area adding a local ingredient to this famous soup.

Serves 4 – 6

INGREDIENTS

Ozoni

500ml **kombu dashi/kelp stock** or **vegetable stock**
2 cups **water**
200g (7oz) **firm tofu** cut into 1.5cm cubes
75g (2.6oz) **carrots**, sliced
2 **spring onions**, sliced
Handful of **fresh baby spinach leaves**, roughly torn
1 Tbsp **soy sauce**

Easy Microwave Mochi / Rice Cake

240g (8.4oz) **glutinous rice flour**
480ml **water**
3 Tbsp **cornflour** for dusting

METHOD

Ozoni

Pour the stock and 2 cups of water into a saucepan and bring to the boil. Add the carrot, tofu and soy sauce to the pot and cook uncovered until the carrot has softened, adding more water if needed. Add the mochi – the amount is entirely up to you. When the mochi is cooked and soft all the way through, add the spring onion and spinach, and let them wilt before serving.

Mochi

Mix the rice flour and water in a medium bowl to create a smooth paste. Cover the bowl with plastic wrap and microwave on high in a 900MW oven for 4 minutes. Let it cool down for 5 - 10 minutes. Remove the plastic wrap, put the mixture on a counter dusted with cornflour and cut into bite-sized shapes.

Cook's Note – The basic volume ratio of rice flour to water is 1:1; use more water for softer mochi – less water for firmer mochi.

Jj
Japan

Grilled Fish & Miso Soup

Serves 2 – 3

INGREDIENTS

Miso Soup
5g (0.2oz) dried wakame/dried seaweed sheets
150g (5.3oz) tofu
2 spring onions, sliced
800ml good-quality vegetable stock
3 Tbsp white or red miso paste

Grilled Fish
salt
2 small-medium whole oily fish, cleaned and deboned.
oil for frying

To Serve
soy sauce
steamed white rice
eggs

A piece of simply grilled fish served with miso soup is a traditional Japanese breakfast. Miso is a paste made with fermented soy beans and barley, or rice malt. When mixed with stock and vegetables, it becomes a delicious savoury broth.

METHOD

Miso Soup
Soak dried wakame/seaweed in water for about 15 minutes to reconstitute it, then drain and set aside. Cut the tofu into 1cm cubes and slice the spring onion diagonally into 2cm pieces.

Heat the stock in a small saucepan over medium heat until boiling. Then, using a soup ladle, remove some stock and place in a small bowl. Add the miso paste and mix well until the paste has dissolved. Put this mixture back into the saucepan with the stock and heat again until boiling. Add the cubes of tofu and wakame/seaweed and sprinkle with the spring onion.

Grilled Fish
Cover a frying pan with foil. Sprinkle salt liberally on both sides of the fish. Heat the frying pan on medium heat and lightly oil the surface of the aluminium foil. Place 1 fish in the pan and cook for 7 - 8 minutes on each side or until the fish is browned and cooked through. Repeat with the second fish.

Serve miso soup and grilled fish piping hot with soy sauce, bowls of steamed white rice and egg, either raw or cooked, according to your preference.

Jj
Jordan

In Jordan, when you're finished drinking your coffee, you must shake your coffee cup from side to side. This means that you have had enough. If you just put your cup down on the table, your host will think you want more and will refill your cup over and over again.

Falafel
Vegetarian

Makes 10 – 15 falafel

INGREDIENTS

410g (14.5oz) tin **chickpeas**
1 **onion**, chopped
2 **leeks**, roughly chopped
3 cloves **garlic**, crushed
2 Tbsp **fresh coriander**, chopped
2 Tbsp **fresh dill**, chopped
2 Tbsp **fresh parsley**, chopped
1 Tbsp **flour**
1 tsp **baking soda**
1 tsp **ground cumin**
½ tsp **cayenne pepper**
salt and **milled black pepper**
oil for frying

To Serve (optional)
Tzatziki
green olives
cherry tomatoes

METHOD

Drain and rinse the chickpeas and set aside. Place the onions, leek, garlic and herbs into a mixing bowl. Add the flour, baking soda, cumin and cayenne pepper. Season well. Add the drained chickpeas and stir well to combine. Put the mixture into the bowl of a food processor and blend until a thick green paste forms. Using a wet spoon, shape the mixture into 2cm x 4cm flat rounds. Heat some oil in a heavy-bottomed pan. Fry the falafel discs over medium heat for 2 - 3 minutes per side or until the falafels are golden and browned on both sides.

Cook's Note – If your falafel breaks in the pan, your mixture may be too moist. To fix this, roll the falafel discs in a little flour before frying.

Jj
Jordan

Ful Medames
Vegetarian, Gluten-free

*Serves 2 by itself or 4
as a dip with pita bread and
other bits and pieces*

INGREDIENTS

410g (14.5oz) tin **fava beans**
(broad beans)*
2 cloves **garlic**, crushed
½ tsp **ground cumin**
pinch of **cayenne pepper**
salt and **black pepper**
1 **lemon**, zest and juice
1 **tomato**, chopped
olive oil
60g (2oz) **fresh parsley**, finely chopped

To Serve (optional)
pita or lavash breads (gluten-free
if required)
grilled vegetables
grilled halloumi cheese
lemon wedges

**Substitute fava beans with butter beans
for a less robust option.*

Ful (pronounced "fool") is Arabic for "beans". This dish is served all over the Middle East; sometimes the beans are left whole and served as a hearty breakfast stew with lemon and garlic, and sometimes, like in this recipe, they are mashed to a rough paste and scooped up with pita bread.

METHOD

Empty the tin of beans – including the liquid – into a large pan and bring to the boil. Turn the heat down and simmer for 10 minutes or until the beans are warmed through.

Remove the beans from the saucepan with a slotted spoon and reserve some of the cooking liquid. Place the beans in a large bowl and roughly mash. Mix the garlic, cumin, cayenne pepper, salt and pepper, lemon zest and juice together in a small bowl. Stir the mixture into the beans. If the mixture is too stodgy, add some of the cooking water to thin it out, but be careful not to make it too mushy. Transfer the beans to a shallow serving dish and top with the chopped tomato, a drizzle of olive oil and the fresh parsley. Serve with fresh and warmed pita or lavash flatbreads, grilled vegetables, grilled halloumi cheese and lemon wedges.

Lithuania

Black bread and salt in Lithuania symbolise good luck and are usually given to people who have just moved into a new house, or a couple that have just gotten married.

Poppy Seed Loaf
Vegetarian

Makes 1 loaf

INGREDIENTS

Dough
500g (17.6oz) flour
180ml milk, warm
1 Tbsp instant dry yeast
100g (3.5oz) sugar
2 eggs

Filling
60g (2oz) glacé fruit, chopped
75g (2.6oz) fruitcake mix
75g (2.6oz) pecan nuts, chopped
60ml smooth apricot jam
75g (2.6oz) butter, melted
75g (2.6oz) poppy seeds

METHOD

Dough
Put half of the flour, the warm milk, yeast and sugar in a large, greased bowl and mix until well combined into a sticky dough. Cover the bowl with plastic wrap and put it in a warm place until the dough has risen and doubled in size.

Beat the eggs and salt and add to the dough in the bowl, along with the remaining flour. Knead until the dough is smooth and elastic, adding some water if necessary. Then put the dough back in the bowl and let it rise again until doubled in size.

Filling
Mix the glacé fruit, fruitcake mix, nuts and jam together. Roll the dough out until 1 - 2cm in thickness onto a lightly-floured surface and brush with melted butter. Sprinkle the poppy seeds onto the dough. Spread the filling over the poppy seeds and roll the dough into a sausage shape, starting at the long end. You can either leave the roll straight or shape it into a ring. Place the dough on a baking tray lined with baking paper and leave to rise until it has doubled in size. At this point, you can also put the loaf in the fridge and bake it later, leaving it to come to room temperature before you do.

Preheat the oven to 190°C. Brush the loaf with the beaten egg and bake for 40 - 50 minutes or until golden brown. Serve warm.

LI
Lithuania

Milk Soup
Vegetarian

Serves 3 – 4

This sweet soup makes a comforting breakfast.

INGREDIENTS

1L **full cream milk**
200g (7oz) (dry weight) **egg noodles**
60g (2oz) **butter**
2 Tbsp **sugar**
½ tsp **salt**

To Serve (any)
butter or cream
cinnamon sugar
honey or maple syrup
stewed apricots
fruit-flavoured jam
nuts

METHOD

Pour the milk and noodles into a medium saucepan and bring to the boil. Once the milk is boiling and the noodles are cooked, take the saucepan off the heat and stir in the butter, sugar and salt.

Serve with your favourite seasonal toppings.

Mm
Malaysia

Malaysia is famous for its durian fruit, which tastes delicious but smells terrible. The stench is so bad that you're not allowed to eat durian fruit in a hotel or on the bus or train. Thank goodness for that!

Chickpea Curry
Vegetarian, Gluten-free

Serves 4 – 6

INGREDIENTS

3 **onions**, thinly sliced
2 **tomatoes**, chopped
1 Tbsp **fresh ginger**, finely grated
1 Tbsp **garlic**, crushed
2 Tbsp **oil**
2 **bay leaves**
5 **cloves**
4 **cardamom pods**
6 **peppercorns**
1 tsp **cumin seeds**
½ tsp **cayenne pepper**
½ tsp **turmeric**
2 tsp **garam masala**
2 x 410g (14.5oz) tins **chickpeas**, drained
salt to taste
250ml **water**
3cm **fresh ginger**, julienned
2 Tbsp **fresh coriander**, chopped

To Serve
naan or flatbreads (gluten-free if required)

METHOD

In a blender or food processor, blend 2 of the onions, the tomatoes, ginger and garlic to form a smooth paste. Heat the oil in a heavy-bottomed pan over medium heat, then add the bay leaves, cloves, cardamom and peppercorns, and fry for about 30 seconds. Add the remaining onion and fry until just golden. Add the tomato-onion paste and fry for another minute or 2. Then add the cumin, cayenne pepper, turmeric and garam masala to the pan and fry for about 5 minutes. Rinse the chickpeas well, add them to the pan and mix to combine. Add salt to taste and enough water to make a gravy – about 250ml. Cover and simmer for 10 minutes. Once the chickpeas have softened, use a flat spoon to mash them roughly, leaving some whole. Mix well and take the pan off the heat. Garnish with the julienned ginger and fresh chopped coriander. Serve piping hot with naan or flatbreads.

Mm
Malaysia

Nasi Lemak
Gluten-free

Serves 8

INGREDIENTS

Rice
500ml coconut milk
500ml water
½ tsp ground ginger
5cm piece fresh ginger, peeled
and thinly sliced
½ tsp salt
1 bay leaf
210g (7.4oz) long grain rice, rinsed
and drained
2 Tbsp oil for frying

Garnishes
250ml sunflower oil
200g (7oz) peanuts
4 eggs, hard-boiled
1 cucumber, sliced
90g (3.2oz) anchovies

Sauce
2 Tbsp oil
1 onion, sliced
3 cloves garlic, thinly sliced
3 shallots or 1 red onion, thinly sliced
2 tsp chilli paste
50g (1.8oz) white anchovies, washed
½ tsp salt
1 Tbsp white sugar
60ml tamarind juice*

This traditional savoury Malaysian breakfast is made up of coconut-flavoured rice with a zesty sauce. It's served with loads of little accompaniments.

METHOD

Rice
Place the coconut milk, water, ground ginger, ginger root, salt, bay leaf and rice into a pan. Cover and bring to the boil. Reduce heat and simmer for 20 - 30 minutes.

Garnishes
Heat the oil in a heavy-bottomed saucepan or wok over medium-high heat. Add the peanuts and cook briefly until lightly browned. Remove the peanuts with a slotted spoon and drain them on a paper towel. Place the pan back on the stove and stir in the anchovies, cooking briefly until they are crispy. Remove with a slotted spoon and drain on a paper towel.

Sauce
Heat the oil in a pan and gently fry the onion, garlic and shallots for 4 - 5 minutes. Add the chilli paste and cook for 10 minutes, stirring occasionally. If the chilli paste is too dry, add a little water. Stir in anchovies and cook for 5 minutes, before adding the salt, sugar and tamarind juice, and simmer until the sauce has thickened. Spoon the rice into bowls and serve with the onion and garlic sauce, and top with peanuts, fried anchovies, hard-boiled eggs and cucumber.

*Soak 2 tablespoons of tamarind paste in 80ml boiling water. Once soft and pulpy, push the mixture through a sieve. The resulting liquid is the tamarind juice.

Mm
Mexico

Mexico leads the world in per capita egg consumption. Breakfast in Mexico is a big deal! It's a long and lingering affair, usually starting with a fresh fruit plate or fruit juice, followed by a big and hearty dish to keep locals fuelled until the early afternoon.

Churros
Vegetarian

*Makes about
24 medium-length churros*

INGREDIENTS

oil for frying
75g (2.6oz) sugar
1 tsp ground cinnamon
75g (2.6oz) butter
2 Tbsp brown sugar
250ml water
½ tsp salt
120g (4.2oz) flour
½ tsp mixed spice
pinch of cayenne pepper (optional)
2 eggs
1 tsp vanilla extract

To Serve (optional)
chocolate sauce or chilli-chocolate sauce

Churros, also known as crullers, are small sausage-shaped morsels of fried dough, similar to doughnuts, deftly and deliciously coated in cinnamon sugar. They are even more delectable when dunked into a warm chilli-spiked chocolate sauce.

METHOD

Heat 3 - 5cm of oil in a deep fat fryer or a medium-sized deep pan. Mix the sugar and ground cinnamon together and place onto a flat dish. Heat the butter, brown sugar, water and salt in a small saucepan and bring to a rapid boil. Remove from heat and beat in the flour, mixed spice and cayenne pepper – this will take a good few minutes and some energetic stirring – until everything is well blended.

In a separate bowl, mix the eggs and vanilla together and add this to the flour mixture. Stir until everything comes together and forms a soft dough. Fill a piping bag with the dough and attach the largest star nozzle you have. Test the oil by dropping a small amount of dough into the pan. If the dough bubbles up straight away, then the oil is hot enough.

Carefully squeeze 8 - 10cm strips of dough into the oil and cook in batches of 3 - 4 churros at a time, for 1 - 2 minutes per side, until the churros are golden brown on all sides. When they're ready, remove with a slotted spoon and drain on a paper towel. Roll the churros in the cinnamon-sugar mixture while they're still warm. Serve at once as they are, or dip into a warm chilli-chocolate sauce.

Mm
Mexico

Huevos Divorciados
Divorced Eggs ~ Gluten-free

This colourful Mexican breakfast is called "divorced eggs" because traditionally, there is a distinct line drawn between two fried eggs using tortilla chips, refried beans or chilaquiles. One egg is covered with "salsa roja", a fiery red sauce and the other is topped with "salsa verde", a cooling green sauce. They represent distinct and complementary (or in the case of divorce, probably conflicting!) flavours.

Serves 4

INGREDIENTS

Salsa Roja (Red Sauce)
4 **plum tomatoes**, cored
½ **onion**, peeled
1 **red** or **green chilli**
60ml good-quality **chicken stock** (gluten-free if required)
salt and **milled black pepper**

Salsa Verde (Green Sauce)
80g (2.8oz) **fresh coriander**, chopped
2 cloves **garlic**, finely chopped
50g (1.8oz) **pine nuts**, toasted
3 Tbsp **Parmesan cheese**, finely grated
125ml **light olive oil** or **peanut oil**
salt and **milled black pepper**

To Serve
4 x 15cm **soft corn tortillas** (gluten-free if required)
oil for shallow frying
4 - 8 **eggs**

> *Cook's Note* – For a colourful breakfast fiesta, make a line through the centre of the tortilla with some favourite Mexican ingredients: refried beans, guacamole, sour cream, grated cheddar cheese, chopped chillies and fresh coriander.

METHOD

Salsa Roja (Red Sauce)
Place the tomatoes, onion and chilli into a hot, dry pan and cook, charring on all sides, turning occasionally, for 5 - 7 minutes. Transfer the charred vegetables into a food processor. While the motor is still running, gradually add the chicken stock and process to form a smooth sauce. Pour the salsa back into the same pan and cook over a medium heat for 5 - 6 minutes or until the sauce turns bright red. Season with salt and pepper to taste.

Salsa Verde (Green Sauce)
Place the coriander, garlic, pine nuts and Parmesan cheese into the bowl of a food processor and pulse until roughly chopped. While the motor is still running, gradually pour the oil as a thin stream into the processor until the ingredients come together to form a rough paste. Season with salt and pepper to taste.

To Serve
Fry the tortillas in a lightly-oiled pan for 30 - 45 seconds per side until they are crispy. Cover the cooked tortillas in foil to keep warm. In the same pan, fry the eggs until done according to your liking (I like them when the yolks have just set but are still soft). Season with sea salt.

Place a warm and crispy tortilla onto a serving plate. Spoon a quarter of each sauce onto opposite sides of the tortilla and top each side with a fried egg. Serve immediately.

Mm
Morocco

One of the most popular sweet treats in Morocco is the Moroccan version of a doughnut. These little pieces of fried dough are found in street stalls rather than bakeries, and instead of putting them into boxes, the stall vendors will thread all the doughnuts you buy onto a piece of string for you to carry home.

Fried Eggs with Cumin & Mint Tea
Vegetarian, Gluten-free

Serves 1 – 2

INGREDIENTS

2 **eggs**
olive oil – enough to cover the bottom of a plate
1 tsp **cumin seeds**

To Serve
olives
pita bread, toasted (gluten-free if required)
creamy white cheese, feta or goat cheese
hot harissa-style sauce (optional)

Mint Tea
60g (2oz) **fresh mint** or **spearmint leaves**, stalks removed
2 tsp **green tea leaves** or 2 **green tea tea bags**
500ml **boiling water**
1 - 2 Tbsp **sugar**, according to taste

To Serve
fresh mint leaves

METHOD

Fried Eggs with Cumin
Pour enough olive oil into a deep plate (or 2 plates) to cover the bottom, along with the cumin seeds. Fry 2 eggs. When the eggs are done, slide them into the olive oil and add olives. Serve immediately with pita bread, cheese and a hot harissa-style sauce, if desired.

Mint Tea
Rinse the mint leaves and place into a teapot with the green tea. Top up the teapot with boiling water. Stir, close the teapot lid and allow to infuse for 4 - 5 minutes. Stir in the sugar to taste. Pour the tea through a strainer into pretty glasses or tea cups and serve with a sprig of mint, if desired.

Cook's Note – The mint tea is also delicious and refreshing served iced. Fill half a glass with the iced tea, add a slice of lime, lots of ice and top up with tonic water, lemonade or sparkling water.

Mm
Morocco

Makes 12 pancakes

INGREDIENTS

Harcha
350g (12.3oz) **fine semolina** (not durum flour)
3 Tbsp **sugar**
2 tsp **baking powder**
½ tsp **salt**
125g (4.4oz) **butter**, softened or melted
120 - 180ml **milk**
60g (2oz) **coarse semolina** (optional)

To Serve
honey
fresh grapes
fresh dates

Harcha
Semolina flatbreads ~ Vegetarian

In Morocco, there are many different kinds of pancakes. These thick little pancakes are made with semolina flour, which is more grainy than normal flour and is sometimes made out of corn instead of wheat.

METHOD

In a mixing bowl, combine the fine semolina, sugar, baking powder and salt. Add the butter and blend just until the mixture is sandy and the semolina grains have all been moistened. Add 120ml of milk and mix until a dough forms. It should be quite moist, wet almost, and easily packed into a large mound. If the mixture is still too dry, add more milk. Shape the dough into medium-sized balls and leave the dough to rest for a few minutes.

Preheat a griddle or medium frying pan over medium-low heat. While the griddle is heating, roll the balls in the coarse semolina (this is optional for appearance and texture) and flatten each ball into a disc just under 1cm in thickness. Cook the harcha over a low heat, about 5 - 10 minutes on each side, until they are a pale to medium-golden in colour. Turn only once and check occasionally to be sure the harcha aren't colouring too quickly, as they need some time to cook all the way through.

Serve with honey or fresh grapes and dates, if desired.

Mm
Mozambique

Watch out for the cucumbers in Mozambique. Unlike Western cucumbers, the Mozambican ones are covered in big, thorny spikes – sharp enough to prick your finger on.

Xima
Maize Porridge ~ Vegetarian, Gluten-free

Maize meal is used in many African dishes, like this thick Mozambican breakfast porridge.

Serves 3 – 4

INGREDIENTS

940ml water
150g (5.3oz) white maize meal or white polenta
4 Tbsp ground almonds
1 Tbps butter
1 tsp vanilla extract

To Serve
butter or mascarpone cheese
ground cinnamon
cashew nuts
honey

Cook's Note – Use half water, half coconut milk as an option.

METHOD

Bring the water to the boil in a large saucepan. Slowly add the maize meal, stirring constantly. Add the ground almonds and continue to stir until the water is absorbed. Bring to the boil, stirring continuously to avoid lumps. Then turn the heat down to a simmer, covering the saucepan loosely. Stir frequently and add more water if required. After about 25 - 30 minutes, the porridge should be ready. Serve with butter, cinnamon, honey and chopped nuts.

Mm
Mozambique

Bolo De Ananás
Pineapple Upside Down Cake ~ Vegetarian

Makes 1 medium-sized cake

INGREDIENTS

Glazed Pineapple
50g (1.8oz) **butter**, softened
50g (1.8oz) **light soft brown sugar**
7 - 8 **pineapple rings** in syrup, drained
and syrup reserved
7 - 8 **glacé cherries**

Cake
100g (3.5oz) **butter**, softened
100g (3.5oz) **caster sugar**
100g (3.5oz) **flour**
1 tsp **baking powder**
1 tsp **vanilla extract**
½ tsp **ground ginger**
2 **eggs**
2 Tbsp **reserved pineapple syrup**

To Serve
fresh cherries

METHOD

Glazed Pineapple
Preheat the oven to 180°C. Brush the base and side of a 23cm cake tin
with butter.

Use an electric beater to beat the butter and brown sugar together until pale and
creamy, and spread over the base of the cake tin. Place the pineapple rings, tightly
packed next to each other, on top of the sugar mixture. Place a halved cherry in the
centre of each ring.

Cake
Place the cake ingredients in a bowl along with 2 tablespoons of the reserved
pineapple syrup and, using an electric whisk, gently beat together. Spoon the batter
on top of the pineapple and smooth it out so it's level. Bake for 30 - 35 minutes
or until a skewer inserted into the centre comes out clean. Run a flat-bladed knife
around the inside edge of the tin. Turn the cake out onto a serving plate. Serve with
fresh cherries.

Nn
Netherlands

If a Dutch person finds that their stomach is grumbling but they have no time to eat at a restaurant, they will probably visit a vending machine. Vending machines in Holland sell more than just chips and sweets. You can buy hot meals from them, like the Dutch version of a hot dog and small potato cakes called croquettes.

Ontbijtkoek
Vegetarian

Makes 1 medium loaf

INGREDIENTS

125g (4.4oz) flour
100g (3.5oz) rye flour
1 Tbsp baking powder
2 tsp cinnamon
½ tsp ground cardamom
½ tsp ground ginger
½ tsp coriander seeds, crushed
½ tsp ground cloves
½ tsp salt
100g (3.5oz) brown sugar
250ml milk
125ml honey
60ml molasses

To Serve
butter
cheese
fresh fruit

Ontbijtkoek means "breakfast cake". This loaf has a spicy flavour and isn't too sweet, making it perfect for breakfast.

METHOD

Preheat the oven to 160°C and grease a 20cm cake tin. Sift the dry ingredients into a large mixing bowl and stir in the sugar. Whisk the milk, honey and molasses together and stir into the dry mixture. Mix until well combined. Place the mixture into the prepared tin and bake for 60 - 70 minutes or until a skewer or tip of a knife inserted into the middle comes out clean. Once cool enough, slice and serve cold, warm, or toasted with plenty of butter, cheese and fresh fruit.

Nn
Netherlands

Toast with Hagelslag
Vegetarian

Serves 4 or more

INGREDIENTS

2 Tbsp **butter**, softened or 3 Tbsp **smooth cream cheese**, softened
4 slices **white** or **fruit bread**
Hagelslag and/or **Muisjes**

To Serve
glass of milk

Traditional Dutch Hagelslag, also known as "toast sprinkles", are available at good supermarkets and Dutch bakeries. They come in an assortment of flavours such as milk and dark chocolate and fruit. Pink and blue anise-flavoured "Muisjes" sprinkles are used to toast the arrival of a new baby. The Dutch are so crazy about Hagelslag that they collectively consume over fourteen million kilos per year!

METHOD

Lightly toast bread, spread with butter and/or cream cheese and sprinkle with generous amounts of your favourite flavoured Hagelslag. Serve with a glass of milk.

Nn
New Zealand

New Zealanders – aka Kiwis – generally enjoy a light, continental-style breakfast. As the country is an archipelago, seafood is a large part of the cuisine and can often be found in breakfast dishes.

Steel-cut Oat Porridge
Vegetarian, Gluten-free

Serves 4

INGREDIENTS

175g (6.2oz) **steel-cut oats** (gluten-free if required)
250ml **water**
500ml **full cream milk***
2 thick strips of **lemon peel**
½ tsp **salt**
pinch of **mixed spice**
1 **vanilla pod**, sliced to release
1 **cinnamon stick** (optional)

To Serve – any
maple syrup, honey or cinnamon sugar, a dollop of thick farm-style cream, caramelized nuts, seasonal poached fruits or apple and cinnamon compote, fresh berries or sliced banana

*Or replace half of the milk with evaporated milk for an ultra-luxurious creamy bowl of comfort food.

METHOD

Place all of the ingredients into a heavy-based saucepan. Stir to combine and bring to the boil. Reduce the heat to the lowest setting and simmer, stirring occasionally, for 25 - 35 minutes, until the oats have softened and the liquid has thickened. Remove the lemon peel, cinnamon stick and vanilla pod, if using, before serving. Serve hot with some of the suggested toppings.

Nn
New Zealand

Kūtai (Mussel) & Potato Fritters

Makes 4 large fritters

INGREDIENTS

500g (17.6oz) or 25 **mussels**
150g (5.3oz) **carrots**, peeled and grated
2 small **sweet potatoes** or **kumara***,
peeled and grated
1 medium **potato**, peeled and grated
½ **onion**, diced
100g (3.5oz) **flour**
1 tsp **baking powder**
salt and **milled black pepper**
3 **eggs**, beaten
oil for frying

To Serve
grilled bacon
lemon wedges
homemade chutney

**Kumara are also known as orange or gold sweet potatoes.*

Right on the edge of a town called Ohakune, you'll find the world's largest carrot statue. The statue was built as a tribute to all the carrot farmers of Ohakune and the town is known as the "carrot capital" of New Zealand. These tasty fritters make for a delicious breakfast.

METHOD

Cook the mussels in salted boiling water for 4 - 5 minutes or until the shells open. Discard any mussels that haven't opened, then remove the mussel meat from the shells, discarding the beards and any grit or dirt, and roughly chop the mussel meat. Place the chopped mussels into a bowl with the carrots, sweet potato, potato and onion, and gently combine. Sift the flour and baking powder over the mussel mixture, season well and fold in the beaten eggs. Mix together until a thick batter is formed. Heat a little oil in a non-stick pan and drop spoonfuls of the mixture into the pan to form fritters (about 3 tablespoons per fritter). Gently fry the fritters for 3 - 4 minutes on each side, until they are golden brown and cooked through. Drain on a paper towel and serve with grilled bacon, lemon wedges and homemade chutney.

Peru

Peru was the first country ever to grow potatoes, and today, they have over three thousand varieties. There is even a Peruvian saying that goes "Soy mas Peruano que la papa", which means, "I am more Peruvian than the potato".

Lomo Saltado
Beef & Tomato Stir Fry ~ Gluten-free

Lomo Saltado is somewhere between a stir fry and a casserole. It's a breakfast that's usually reserved for weekends and traditionally served with both white rice and French fries.

METHOD

Season the beef with garlic, salt and pepper. Heat the oil in a wok or large pan over a very high heat. Stir fry the meat in batches – so it browns rather than steams – for about 5 - 6 minutes a batch, depending on how hot the stove is. Once all batches are browned, put all the meat back into the pan. Add the onion, tomato and chilli to the pan and stir for about 2 - 3 minutes. The tomatoes and onions should be crunchy, not mushy. Stir in the soy sauce and vinegar. Add the beef stock and bring to the boil for a few minutes. Season with salt and pepper. Remove the pan or wok from the heat, add the chopped coriander and serve immediately with French fries and white rice.

Serves 4

INGREDIENTS

400g (14.1oz) **sirloin steak**, cut into thin slices
2 cloves **garlic**, finely diced
salt and **milled black pepper**
3 Tbsp **oil**
1 small **red onion**, sliced
2 **tomatoes**, sliced
1 - 2 **red chillies**, seeded and sliced
2 Tbsp **soy sauce**
3 Tbsp **red wine vinegar**
80ml good quality **beef stock**
1⅓ Tbsp **fresh coriander**, roughly chopped

To Serve
French fries
white rice

Pp
Peru

Caldo de Gallina

Serves 6 – 8

INGREDIENTS

2 **leeks**, trimmed and sliced
2 **celery sticks**, sliced
2 **carrots**, peeled and sliced
6 **baby potatoes**, halved
3cm piece **ginger**, peeled
and finely grated
2 cloves **garlic**, crushed
1.5L **chicken stock**
800g (28.2oz) **skinless, boneless chicken thighs**, roasted and chopped
100g (3.5oz) **dried egg noodles**
salt and **milled black pepper**

To Serve
hard-boiled eggs, quartered (optional)
2 Tbsp fresh coriander, chopped
4 spring onions, thinly sliced
2 limes, quartered
1 fresh red chilli, seeded and finely
chopped (optional)

Caldo De Gallina means "Hen Soup". It's a rich
chicken soup, common at the Peruvian breakfast table.

METHOD

Place the leeks, celery, carrots, potatoes, ginger, garlic and the
chicken stock into a large heavy-bottomed saucepan. Bring to
the boil over high heat then reduce heat to simmer and cook for
30 minutes. Add the roasted chicken and the egg noodles and
cook until the noodles are just tender – 6 - 8 minutes. Season
soup with salt and pepper. Divide the soup between 6 - 8
deep serving bowls. Garnish each portion with eggs (if using)
and some of the coriander, spring onion, limes and chilli.
Serve immediately.

Pp
Portugal

Portugal holds the world record for the longest ever dinner table. The table was made on a bridge for a presidential celebration, and it was big enough to seat fifteen thousand people.

Pastéis de Nata
Custard Tarts ~ Vegetarian

Makes 12 tarts

INGREDIENTS

Dough

350g (12.3oz) frozen puff pastry, defrosted
1 tsp ground cinnamon
pinch of ground nutmeg
80g (2.8oz) caster sugar

Filling

180ml milk
100g (3.5oz) caster sugar
1 tsp vanilla essence
1 strip lemon peel (use a vegetable peeler)
125ml cream
3 large eggs, whisked
2 Tbsp flour

METHOD

Dough

Preheat the oven to 220°C. Grease a 12 cup muffin tin with butter or non-stick spray. Mix the cinnamon, nutmeg and caster sugar together. Unroll the pastry and sprinkle the cinnamon sugar over it. Starting at the long end, tightly roll up the pastry into a log and slice into 12 equal pieces. Place the pieces flat on a board and roll them out into flat disks, big enough to fit into the cups of the muffin tin. The sides should come up a little bit to form a cup.

Filling

Place the milk, caster sugar, vanilla, lemon peel and cream into a small pan. Whisk in the egg and flour. Cook over moderate heat for 5 minutes, whisking constantly, until the mixture thickens and forms a custard. Remove the lemon peel and pour the custard into the pastry cases. Bake for 12 - 15 minutes until the pastry is cooked and the custard is speckled-brown.

Pp
Portugal

Honey Bread
Vegetarian

Makes 1 big loaf

INGREDIENTS

90g (3.2oz) **dried cranberries**
170g (6oz) good-quality **mixed glacé fruit**
such as pear and orange peel, chopped
60ml **port**
150g (5.3oz) **walnuts**
560g (19.8oz) **flour**
1 tsp **salt**
1 tsp **baking soda**
½ tsp **ground cinnamon**
pinch of **ground cloves**
200g (7oz) **sugar**
285g (10oz) **unsalted butter**, plus extra
for greasing
3 large **eggs**
3 tsp **instant dried yeast**
60ml **warm water**
175ml **molasses**
115ml **honey**

To Serve
hard cheese

METHOD

Preheat the oven to 160°C and grease a loaf tin. Place the cranberries, glacé fruit and port into a pan and bring to the boil. Remove from heat, cover and set aside. Pulse the walnuts in a food processor until coarsely chopped. Add the flour, salt, baking soda and spices to the walnuts and pulse quickly to combine. In a separate large bowl or free-standing electric mixer, beat the butter and sugar until pale and fluffy. Add the eggs one at a time, beating well after each addition. In a small bowl, mix the yeast and warm water and leave until the mixture foams. Set aside. Add a third of the flour and walnut mixture to the creamed butter and sugar and beat until combined. Then add the molasses and beat again. Add another third of the remaining flour mix and beat to combine. Then add the honey and beat again. Add the yeast and all of the remaining flour, and mix well. Stir in the glacé fruit mixture. Transfer the batter to the loaf tin and smooth out the top. Bake on the middle shelf of the oven for 50 - 60 minutes or until a toothpick or knife inserted comes out clean. When the loaf is ready, leave to cool on a rack for 10 minutes before removing from the loaf tin. Serve the sweet fruit bread with your favourite cheese.

Rr
Russia

If you ever make an omelette in Russia, don't be surprised if the eggs have adverts on them. Egg companies use special dot printers to write short messages on the shells of the eggs, advertising cars, clothes and everything in-between.

Draniki
Russian Potato Pancakes ~ Vegetarian

Serves 4 – 6

INGREDIENTS

630g (22.2oz) **mashed potatoes**
240g (8.5oz) **mozzarella cheese**, grated
1 **egg**
2 Tbsp **flour**
salt and **pepper**
oil for frying

To Serve
sour cream
chives
smoked salmon slices (non-vegetarian option)

METHOD

In a large bowl, combine the mashed potatoes, mozzarella, egg and flour. Mix well. Heat about 45ml of oil in a heavy-bottomed pan. Take heaped tablespoons of the potato mixture, roll into balls and gently flatten each ball to make a patty. Fry each patty for 3 minutes either side until they're golden brown. Once they're cooked, remove the patties from the pan and place them on a paper towel to soak up any excess oil. Serve with sour cream, chives and smoked salmon (optional).

Rr
Russia

Kasha
Vegetarian, Gluten-free

Serves 2 – 3

INGREDIENTS

70g (2.5oz) **wholegrain buckwheat groats**
1 **egg**, lightly whisked
40g (1.4oz) + 40g + 40g **butter**
3 **onions**, chopped
2 cloves **garlic**, finely crushed
½ tsp **paprika** or **smoked paprika**
salt and **milled black pepper**
500ml **water** or good quality **vegetable stock** (gluten-free if required)
250g (8.8oz) **assorted mushrooms***, roughly chopped or sliced
2 Tbsp **flat-leaf parsley**, finely chopped
1 Tbsp **chives**, finely chopped
fresh dill for garnish

*exotic mushrooms will further enhance the kasha.

Kasha is a thick, savoury porridge that makes a perfect breakfast or late brunch for an icy-cold winter morning.

METHOD

Place the groats and egg into a heavy-bottomed pan and stir the mixture over low-medium heat to remove some of the moisture. Once the mixture has dried out and is slightly brown, add 40g butter, the water or stock, paprika, salt and pepper. Stir to combine, then cover and leave to simmer for 20 minutes over low heat. Remove from the heat and keep warm.

Melt another 40g of butter in a pan and gently fry the onions and garlic for 5 - 6 minutes or until transparent. Add the reserved porridge mixture and mix well. In another pan, melt the remaining 40g butter and sauté the mushrooms for 3 - 4 minutes. Stir the mushrooms, parsley and chives into the savoury porridge and serve warm.

Cook's Note – Not strictly traditional, but a dollop of crème fraiche and some crispy bacon rashers (non-vegetarian), elevates this rustic dish into something special.

Ss
Scotland

In one fun Easter tradition in Scotland, everyone paints and decorates an egg and lets it tumble down the hill to see whose egg can roll the furthest without cracking.

Poached Haddock with Spinach

Serves 4

INGREDIENTS

675g (23.8oz) **smoked haddock**
150ml good-quality **fish** or **vegetable stock**
3 Tbsp **butter**
3 Tbsp **flour**
125g (4.4oz) **white cheddar**, or similar, **cheese**
salt and **milled black pepper**

To Serve

2 Tbsp butter
250g (8.8oz) spinach, chopped
pinch freshly grated nutmeg
4 - 8 eggs (1 or 2 eggs per person, poached)
vinegar for poaching

METHOD

Cut the haddock into 4 pieces and place into a deep pan. Pour the fish stock and milk over the haddock to cover and bring to the boil. Reduce the heat, cover and simmer for 4 - 5 minutes.

Take the pan off the heat, remove the fish using a slotted spoon and keep warm. Strain and reserve the poaching liquid and keep warm. In another pan, melt the butter then stir in and cook the flour until a smooth paste forms. Gradually add the warm poaching liquid, stirring continuously until the sauce thickens. Add the cheese, stirring until all of the cheese has melted. Season and remove from the heat.

To serve, melt the butter in a pan and cook the spinach on low heat until wilted. Season with nutmeg. Poach the eggs according to your liking by breaking them into a boiling saucepan of water with a good splash of vinegar, and removing them with a slotted spoon when cooked.

Arrange the haddock and spinach onto serving plates, pour the cheese sauce over the fish and top with 1 or 2 poached eggs. Serve at once.

Ss
Scotland

Tattie Scones
Vegetarian

Makes 16 scones

INGREDIENTS

500g (17.6oz) **mashed potatoes**
2 Tbsp **butter**, melted, plus extra
for greasing
½ tsp **salt**
1 medium **egg**
125g (4.4oz) **flour**, plus a little extra
for rolling
1 tsp **baking powder**

To Serve
whisky-enriched marmalade
or apricot jam
freshly-whipped cream

"Tattie" is the Scottish word for potato, and these moreish potato cakes are delicious served hot with a traditional fry up, along with a slice of black pudding. They are sublime served with smoked salmon slices and cream cheese, but our favourite has to be served with jam and cream, and a nice strong cup of tea.

METHOD

Preheat the oven to 200°C. Place the mashed potatoes, melted butter, salt, egg, flour and baking powder into a mixing bowl and mix until a sticky dough forms. Roll the dough out onto a floured work surface until it is 1 - 2cm thick. Cut into 4 saucer-sized rounds and make a cross in each round to mark 4 equal wedges. Place the scones onto a greased baking tray and bake for 15 minutes until the scones have risen and turned golden brown. The scones can also be cooked on the stove in a heavy-based frying pan for 5 minutes on either side until golden and risen. To serve, break into wedges, spread with marmalade or jam and serve with cream.

Ss
South Africa

If you see "Monkey Gland Steak" on a South African menu, don't worry – it has nothing to do with real monkeys. Monkey Gland is actually a traditional sweet-tangy sauce, similar to barbecue sauce, and it's usually poured onto steak or chicken.

Vetkoek
Fat Cakes also known as "Magwinya" ~ Vegetarian

A vetkoek (pronounced "feht-cook") is a cross between a doughnut and a bread roll. Traditionally, each vetkoek is split open after cooking and stuffed with a savoury mince filling or a combination of apricot jam and grated cheddar cheese.

Makes 6 – 8

INGREDIENTS

250ml **lukewarm water**
1 Tbsp packet **instant yeast**
875g (30.9oz) **flour**
2 tsp **salt**
3 Tbsp **sugar**
oil for deep fat frying

To Serve

sweet: apricot or strawberry jam
savoury: curried or savoury mince
(non-vegetarian)

METHOD

Pour the lukewarm water into a small jug and sprinkle over the yeast. Leave the mixture for a few minutes until foamy. In a large bowl, combine the flour, salt and sugar. Pour the yeast into the bowl and stir to combine. Add a little more lukewarm water to the dough in small amounts, mixing after each addition, until a soft dough – similar to bread dough – forms.

Place the dough in an electric mixer and use the dough hook to knead until the dough starts coming away from the sides of the mixing bowl. If you don't have an electric mixer, knead by hand for about 15 minutes. Cover the dough with a damp cloth or plastic wrap that's been brushed with oil and leave in a warm place for about an hour, until the dough has risen and doubled in size. Brush your hands with a little oil and roll the dough into golf ball-sized balls.

Heat the oil in a deep fat fryer or heavy-bottomed pan over medium heat. The oil is hot enough when a small piece of dough that is dropped into it immediately bubbles and rises to the surface. Fry the vetkoek in batches, turning often until they're golden brown and cooked through. Remove from the pan with a slotted spoon and drain on a paper towel. Serve with sweet or savoury fillings as desired.

Ss
South Africa

Maltabella
Malted porridge ~ Vegetarian, Gluten-free

Serves 3 – 4

INGREDIENTS

130g (4.6oz) **fine grain sorghum**
250ml **cold water**
450ml **boiling water**
½ tsp **salt**

To Serve
butter and/or cream
ground cinnamon
brown sugar, golden syrup or honey

METHOD

Put the sorghum, cold water and salt in a heavy-based saucepan and mix until the salt has dissolved. Add boiling water, stirring continuously as the porridge thickens. Bring to the boil over medium heat. Turn the heat down slightly and leave the porridge to simmer for 15 - 20 minutes, stirring often.

Serve with butter and/or cream, ground cinnamon, and brown sugar, golden syrup or honey.

Ss
Switzerland

The Swiss sure love their cheese – they consume over twenty-one kilos of cheese per person, per year!

Rösti
Gluten-free

Serves 6 – 8

INGREDIENTS

1.3 kg (3lbs) **potatoes**
(about 4 large ones)
2 Tbsp **butter**
1½ Tbsp **olive oil**
4 Tbsp **kosher salt**, plus more to taste

To Serve
sausages of your choice, cooked
(gluten-free if required)

METHOD

Place potatoes in a large saucepan, cover them with cold water and bring to the boil over medium-high heat. Cook until the potatoes are tender – about 30 minutes. Then drain the potatoes and set aside to cool for about 10 minutes. Peel potatoes and refrigerate until chilled – at least 1 hour. Grate the potatoes using a cheese grater. Set aside.

Heat the butter and oil in a 20cm non-stick heavy-based pan over medium heat. When the butter has melted, add the potatoes, sprinkle with salt and mix well, coating the potatoes in the oil and butter. Gently press the potatoes down with a spatula, using the pan to shape them. Cook for about 20 minutes or until the edges are golden brown, shaking the pan occasionally. Once the potatoes are cooked, cover the pan with a large plate and flip the pan upside down so the rösti lands on the plate.

Then slide the rösti back into the pan, uncooked side down, and cook for a further 20 minutes or until golden brown. Cut into wedges and serve immediately with sausages.

Ss
Switzerland

Bircher Muesli
Vegetarian, Gluten-free

Serves 4

INGREDIENTS

150g (5.3oz) **rolled oats** (gluten-free
if required)
400ml **milk**
60ml **apple juice**
3 Tbsp **lemon juice**
1 large **apple**, cored and grated with peel
1 - 2 Tbsp **honey**
375g (13.2oz) **plain yoghurt**
pinch of **cinnamon**

To Serve
berries or fresh seasonal fruits
chopped nuts

This famous breakfast dish was invented by Dr Maximilian Bircher-Benner, a Swiss physician who believed that eating raw food was very good for your health.

METHOD

Mix the oats, milk, apple juice and lemon juice together and refrigerate overnight.

In the morning, grate the apple and add to the oat mixture, together with the honey, yoghurt and cinnamon, and mix well.

Serve with your favourite fruit and nut toppings.

Uu
United States of America

The first pancakes were called Alita Dolcia ("another sweet" in Latin) and were made by Romans in the first century AD. In the U.S.A., Southerners eat the most pancakes, accounting for a third of the country's pancake consumption.

American Pancakes

Vegetarian

Makes 12 – 16 small pancakes

INGREDIENTS

1 Tbsp **baking powder**
½ tsp **salt**
1 tsp **white sugar**
225g (8oz) **flour**
2 large **eggs**, beaten
2 Tbsp **butter**, melted and cooled
300ml **milk**
butter and **oil** for frying

To Serve
fresh blueberries or bananas
maple or golden syrup
whipped cream or thick
Greek-style yoghurt

METHOD

The easiest way to make these is to put all the ingredients into a blender and blitz. But if you do mix up the batter by hand in a bowl, make a well in the flour, baking powder, salt and sugar then beat in the eggs, melted butter and milk, and transfer to a jug: it's much easier to pour the batter into the pan than to spoon it.

Heat a smooth griddle or pan on the stove.

Use about ¼ cup batter for each pancake. When you cook the pancakes, all you need to remember is that when the upper side of the pancake is blistering and bubbling, it's time to cook the second side. The second side only needs about 1 minute, if that.

Uu
United States of America

Hash Browns
Vegetarian, Gluten-free

Makes 3 medium hash browns

INGREDIENTS

200 - 300g (7 - 10.5oz) **potato**
1 small **onion**
salt and **milled black pepper**
1 Tbsp **butter**
2 tsp **oil**

To Serve

tomato sauce
corned beef
avocado and tomato salsa
chives, to garnish

Originally, "hashed brown potatoes" were simply small patties made from grated potato, then fried. Nowadays, they can include onions and other ingredients. They are popular breakfast fare at diners throughout North America and are known simply as hash browns. They go well with almost any fried or grilled breakfast sides.

METHOD

Line a large bowl with a clean dishcloth. Peel the potato and onion and grate them directly into the bowl. Then remove the moisture from the potato and onion by bundling it up in the dishcloth and twisting the neck to wring out any excess liquid. Twist and squeeze until you've removed as much liquid as possible. Season with salt and pepper.

Heat the butter and oil in a heavy-bottomed pan over medium heat. Add the mixture to the pan and toss lightly until the gratings are coated in butter. Divide the grated potato mixture into separate hash browns and flatten each one with a spatula so the side in contact with the pan gets brown and crispy. Cook until each hash brown is golden brown on each side – about 3 - 4 minutes on the first side and 2 - 3 minutes after you've flipped it. Work gently with the hash browns and try not to move them around too much during cooking, otherwise they'll break.

Serve immediately with tomato sauce, slices of fried corned beef or an avocado and tomato salsa. Garnish with chives.

Vietnam

All dishes are communal in Vietnam and are meant to be shared in the middle of the table. It is customary for the younger generation to ask the elders to eat first. The louder your slurping sounds, the more you're indicating how much you like the food – go on, give it a try, I know that you want to!

Chicken Banh Mi
Vietnamese Chicken Sandwich

Serves 4

INGREDIENTS

225g (7.9oz) **daikon** (radish), peeled – alternatively, use finely shredded cabbage
1 **carrot**, peeled
125ml **rice vinegar**
1 Tbsp **sugar**
½ tsp **salt**
1 x 60cm **baguette**
1 Tbsp **sesame oil**
1 Tbsp **Thai fish sauce**
1 tsp **soy sauce**
1 small tub **chicken liver pâté**
½ **red onion** or **brown onion**, thinly sliced
3 Tbsp **fresh coriander**
2 **cooked chicken breasts** from a rotisserie chicken, thinly sliced*
a few **lettuce leaves**, torn
2 Tbsp good-quality **mayonnaise**

*Alternatively, use smoked chicken breasts.

METHOD

Preheat the oven to 180°C. Shred the radish and carrot in a food processor fitted with a medium shredding disk. Mix the vinegar, sugar and salt together in a mixing bowl. Add the shredded vegetables, toss together and let this stand for 15 minutes, stirring occasionally.

Heat the baguette on the middle rack in the oven until crusty – about 5 minutes. Watch it carefully as it can brown quickly. Cut off each end of the baguette, then slice down the middle, leaving a small "hinge" so it stays intact.

Combine the oil, fish sauce and soy sauce, and brush onto the inside of the baguette. Spread the pâté on the bottom layer of the baguette and top it with the onion, coriander, chicken and lettuce. Drain the slaw in a colander and arrange on top of the lettuce. Spread the top layer of bread with mayonnaise and slice the baguette into sandwiches.

Vietnam

Pho
Beef Noodle Soup

Serves 4 – 6

INGREDIENTS

Broth
1.2L good quality **beef stock**
2 **carrots**, peeled and julienned
4 thick slices **fresh ginger**, peeled
and sliced into matchsticks
1 **cinnamon stick**
3 **star anise**
5 whole **cloves**
2 cloves **garlic**
2 tsp **black peppercorns**
3 Tbsp **Thai fish sauce**

Accompaniments
200g (7oz) **rice noodles**,
cooked as per packet instructions
250g (8.8oz) **seared beef fillet**,
sliced into wafer-thin strips
3 **spring onions**, sliced
250g (8.8oz) **fresh bean sprouts**
and/or **mixed sprouts**
1 Tbsp **fresh coriander**, roughly chopped
1 bunch **fresh basil**, roughly chopped
1 **red pepper**, deseeded
and sliced into strips
2 **limes**, cut into wedges
garlic chives (optional, to serve)

Pronounced "fuh", this light Vietnamese noodle broth
has become a much-loved classic all around the globe.

METHOD

Pour the stock into a large saucepan, along with the carrots, ginger,
cinnamon, star anise, cloves, garlic and peppercorns. Bring to the
boil, then cover and reduce heat to a simmer for 15 - 20 minutes.
Stir in the fish sauce and strain the broth by pouring it through a
sieve or fine colander.

To serve, ladle the hot broth into bowls, arrange the beef, onion,
bean sprouts, coriander, basil, red pepper, lime wedges and
noodles on a platter and serve alongside the broth. Garnish with
garlic chives, if desired.

CONTRIBUTORS

NL
Nina Lewis
Front cover

Breakfast Beans on Toast
Vegetarian

Serves 4

INGREDIENTS

1 Tbsp **olive oil**
2 cloves **garlic**, crushed
1 **onion**, finely chopped
3 **ripe tomatoes**, skinned and finely chopped
2 Tbsp **tomato paste**
1 tsp **dried oregano**
2 Tbsp **wholegrain mustard**
410g (14.5oz) tin **baked beans**
410g (14.5oz) tin **butter beans**
3 Tbsp **Italian parsley**

To Serve
rye bread toast

METHOD

In a saucepan, heat the olive oil then cook the garlic and onion until soft but not browned. Add tomatoes, tomato paste, oregano and mustard and simmer for 5 - 10 minutes. Add beans, stirring until hot. Stir in parsley, season and serve on toast.

Vanessa Lewis
Author, Photographer

CONTRIBUTORS

Vanessa has been photographing food for the past fifteen years and her camera has taken her from Shinjuku to Oaxaca to Paul Bocuse's kitchen. Travel and food assignments have allowed her to see and taste the world. Her family knows not to eat their food before she has snapped a photo on her iPhone and uploaded it to her Instagram – a foodie's visual diary. She has photographed various cookbooks but this is her first time as an author, where she enjoyed complete creative freedom to create a beautiful and functional cookbook with a difference.

www.vanessa-lewis.com | Instagram: vanessalewis

Black Sticky Rice with Coconut
Vegetarian, Gluten-free

Black sticky rice is a lovely wholegrain alternative to white rice, which is the norm in Thailand. Black sticky rice is unpolished sticky rice, meaning the bran has not been removed. It is purplish-black in colour and has a chewy texture.

Serves 4

INGREDIENTS

200g (7oz) **black rice**
500ml **water**
70g (2.5oz) **palm sugar**, grated
1 tsp **vanilla extract**
½ tsp **salt**
125ml **coconut milk**, plus extra for drizzling

To Serve
fresh desiccated coconut* (optional)

METHOD

Soak the rice in plenty of cold water for 1 hour, then drain and rinse the rice well under cold, running water. Place the drained rice into a pan with 500ml of water and bring to the boil, stirring occasionally. Reduce the heat to low and cover and simmer for 30 - 35 minutes. Stir in the palm sugar, coconut milk, vanilla extract and salt. Mix well and simmer uncovered for another 10 - 12 minutes. Remove from the heat and allow the rice to cool before serving. Drizzle extra coconut milk or coconut cream around the rice and serve with fresh desiccated coconut, if desired.

*Fresh or tinned lychees or mango could also be a refreshing option.

JE
Jodie Ennik
Fashion Stylist

CONTRIBUTORS

Jodie's passion for fashion started at an early age. A model at sixteen, she went on to become a fashion stylist at twenty-three and has been adding beauty to advertising campaigns and fashion pages ever since.

Jodie opened Lampost in 2008 – an award-winning photographic production company and creative agency servicing both local and international clients and representing high-end fashion stylists, photographers and make-up artists.

www.lampost.co.za | Instagram: lampostsa

Berry Compote
Vegetarian, Gluten-free

Serves 4

INGREDIENTS

1 Tbsp **butter**
3 Tbsp **caster sugar**
2 Tbsp **orange juice**
1 tsp **vanilla extract**
350g (12.3oz) **frozen mixed berries**, defrosted

To Serve
pancakes
thick cream

METHOD

Melt the butter in a pan over a low heat. Stir in the orange juice, sugar and vanilla extract, and cook, stirring, for 2 - 3 minutes or until the sugar melts. Add in the defrosted berries and any juice. Stir gently and cook for 2 - 3 minutes until the fruit starts to soften. Serve warm with pancakes and thick cream for an indulgent breakfast.

> *Cook's Note* – The compote makes an easy and eye-catching dessert when served on top of a cream-filled pavlova base.

TJ
Taryne Jakobi
Food Stylist

CONTRIBUTORS

Once upon a time, Taryne met a kind lady who ran a food magazine. The lady needed a food stylist. The lady and Taryne had been at Hotel School together, so the lady knew Taryne's credentials were good. She hired Taryne and introduced Taryne to photographer Vanessa Lewis. Six recipe books later – countless editorial articles, impressive advertising campaigns and a never-ending love affair with food – the rest, as they say, is history.

www.tarynejakobi.co.za | Instagram: tarynejakobistyling

Bacon-wrapped Chicken & Potato Hash Browns

A real winner for a Sunday brunch.

Serves 4 – 6

INGREDIENTS

650g (22.9oz) **potatoes**, peeled
1 Tbsp **oil**, plus more for frying
1 Tbsp **butter**, plus more for frying
1 **onion**, finely chopped
2 **spring onions**, thinly sliced
2 cloves **garlic**, crushed
350g (12.3oz) **cooked chicken**
3 Tbsp **flat-leaf parsley**, chopped
1 **egg**
1 Tbsp **wholegrain mustard**
sea salt and freshly **ground black pepper**
8 slices **streaky bacon**
2 Tbsp **seasoned flour** for dusting

To Serve
fresh rocket leaves
tomato salsa
sour cream

> *Cook's Note* – The secret to keeping hash browns together is to not have large chunky ingredients in the mixture. Ensure that the onions etc. are very tender.

METHOD

Cut the potatoes into chunks and cook in boiling water until tender. Drain and return to the heat to steam off any excess moisture. Transfer the potatoes to a bowl and mash roughly with a fork. Heat the oil and butter in a frying pan and cook the onion, spring onions and garlic until very tender – about 6 - 8 minutes. Stir in the potatoes, remove from the heat and allow to cool. Remove the meat off the chicken and discard the skin, bones and any fat. Chop the chicken and add to the potato mixture with the flat-leaf parsley. Whisk the egg and mustard together and add to the mixture. Season with salt and pepper and use a fork to combine everything together. Using floured hands, divide the mixture into 8 portions and form into hash browns approximately 8cm wide and 4 - 5cm high. Wrap a rasher of bacon around the middle of each hash brown and secure using a toothpick. The hash browns can be covered and refrigerated overnight at this point, if desired. To cook, heat a little oil and butter in a frying pan and lightly dust both sides of each hash brown with flour. Cook for 3 - 4 minutes per side or until golden, crispy and piping hot. Alternatively, the hash browns can be browned on both sides, then transferred to a lined baking tray and baked at 180°C for 10 minutes. To serve, place 2 hash browns on each plate and garnish with rocket. Serve with bowls of tomato salsa and sour cream.

AS
Amy Searll
Writer

CONTRIBUTORS

Amy started out working as a copywriter in advertising, but she soon realised that her true love was food, and writing about food became her favourite thing to do. She has since written for magazines like Nicework, Crush and the Mahala online lifestyle portal, as well as various food brands. Amy also blogs regularly about her kitchen adventures, voicing her rather strong opinions on all things food.

www.amythinksfood.blogspot.com

Marmalade
Vegetarian

Makes 1 jar

INGREDIENTS

1 medium **orange***, with the thinnest peel possible
100g (3.5oz) **sugar**
2 Tbsp **water**
1 tsp **crystallized ginger**, finely chopped

Marmalade is best served on hot, golden toasted bread with lashings of butter. It also makes a great topping on toasted crumpets, hot cross buns, scones and muffins. Don't forget to serve alongside a nice cup of tea.

METHOD

Wash the orange thoroughly and pat dry. Cut off both ends of the orange and cut in half, then roughly cut each half into slices. Place the sliced oranges into the bowl of a food processor and pulse until the peel is very finely chopped. Transfer the orange mixture to a pan and add the sugar, water and ginger. Stir and bring the mixture to a gentle boil. Cook, boiling for 15 minutes, stirring frequently. Allow the mixture to cool and then transfer to a sterilized jar, fitted with a tight lid. Keep the marmalade in the fridge and use as required.

*If the orange is very large, then double the amount of water and sugar.

AD
Alek Daray
Hair Stylist

Alek has worked as a session stylist and hairdresser for the last three years, after being mentored by some of the greatest stylists in South Africa. Freelancing as a session stylist for the advertising and fashion industries, Alek currently works on Kloof Street, Cape Town.

Simplified Sourdough
Vegetarian

Makes 1 medium loaf

INGREDIENTS

405g (14.3oz) **bread flour**
1½ tsp **salt**
¼ tsp **instant dry yeast** (if fermenting for 18 hours), or ¾ tsp **instant dry yeast** (if fermenting for 6 hours)
385g (14oz) + 30g (1oz) **unsweetened plain yoghurt** (if needed), containing active cultures

METHOD

Mix the bread flour, yeast, salt and 385g plain yoghurt in the bowl of a free-standing electric mixer fitted with a dough hook, on a medium-low speed for 2 minutes, until a dough forms. You can also mix this by hand in a large bowl. If the dough is too dry and has difficulty coming together, add the additional plain yoghurt. Knead the dough on a medium-low speed, or with your hands, for a few minutes until it becomes springy. The dough should be very sticky but able to retain its shape. Cover the bowl with plastic wrap and let the dough double in size and ferment at room temperature for a minimum of 6 hours or, preferably, 18 hours with a maximum 20 hours.

After fermentation, transfer the dough to a flour-dusted counter top. Use just enough flour to prevent the dough from sticking. Fold the dough gently over itself like a letter, being careful not to crush the air bubbles inside. Turn 90° and fold again. Shape the dough into a large ball. Transfer the dough to a piece of floured baking paper and cover with a large bowl. Leave to prove again for 1 - 2 hours. After 45 minutes, preheat the oven to 225°C. The dough is ready when it has doubled in size again and doesn't spring back when pressed. Lift the dough using the baking paper and place it with the paper in a Dutch oven or large ovenproof pot. Cover with a lid and bake for 30 minutes. Remove the lid and bake until the crust is golden brown. Let the loaf cool on a rack for 20 minutes before slicing and serving.

EvR
Elena van Renen
Graphic Designer

CONTRIBUTORS

Elena's passion for food and design was influenced by her Sicilian father, her Italian mother's cooking and her parents' furniture design company.

Elena spent ten years immersed in the design business at a branding and design agency called The New Black, before branching out, launching a freelance design career and cooking meals infused with her Italian spirit.

www.elenavanrenen.com

Fried Nutella & Banana Ravioli
Vegetarian

Serves 4 – 6

INGREDIENTS

1 medium **banana**, peeled and cut into 6mm pieces to yield about 130g (4.6oz)
55g (1.9oz) **light brown sugar**
40g (1.4oz) **walnuts**, finely chopped
16 **wonton wrappers**
1 **egg**, beaten
100g (3.5oz) **Nutella**
vegetable oil for frying

Growing up with a mother that cooked Italian food meant that some mornings it was chocolate for breakfast – anything with Nutella!

METHOD

In a small bowl, combine the banana, sugar and walnuts. Using a pastry brush, lightly brush the edges of each wonton wrapper with water. Put about a teaspoon of the Nutella spread in the center of each wrapper and top with 1 - 2 teaspoons of the banana mixture. Fold 1 corner of each won ton wrapper diagonally over the filling to form a triangle. Press the edges together to seal and refrigerate the ravioli for 15 minutes.

Fill a large heavy-bottomed saucepan with about 2cm of the oil. Heat over medium heat until a deep-frying thermometer inserted in the oil reaches about 190° C (If you don't have a thermometer, a cube of bread will brown in about 2 minutes). Fry the ravioli 2 - 3 at a time, turning occasionally until golden – about 60 - 70 seconds. Drain on paper towels. Cool for 2 minutes and serve warm.

LW
Lyn Woodward
Proof Reader and Researcher

CONTRIBUTORS

Lyn is a food stylist, recipe developer and tester, Cape Wine Master and globetrotter. With over 20 years' experience in the culinary field, Lyn has a lot of practical knowledge to add to the creative food styling aspects of her career. "Basically I love anything that revolves around food, wine and travel – especially when they are all combined together!" says Lyn, who is at her happiest when wandering around a food market in some exotic location off the beaten track.

Toasted English Muffins with Ricotta & Figs & Very Berry Smoothie
Vegetarian

Serves 2

INGREDIENTS

Muffins
1 Tbsp **flaked almonds**
2 **English muffins** or crumpets, halved
200g (7oz) **ricotta cheese**
3-4 **fresh figs**, quartered
50g (1.8oz) **fresh raspberries**
2 - 4 Tbsp **maple syrup** (the real stuff!)
1 Tbsp shelled **pistachio nuts**, chopped
2 Tbsp **halva**, crumbled (optional)

Smoothie
250g (8.8oz) **frozen mixed berries**
60g (2oz) **cooked beetroot**, cooled
1 - 2 Tbsp **rose-flavoured syrup**
125ml **thick plain yoghurt**

METHOD

Muffins
Place the almonds in a hot, dry pan and dry fry for 1 minute or until lightly toasted. Set aside to cool. Toast the English muffins. Divide the ricotta cheese between the muffin halves and top with fresh figs, raspberries and a drizzle of maple syrup. Scatter the toasted almonds, pistachio nuts and halva, if using, over the top. Serve at once.

Smoothie
Place all the ingredients into a high-speed blender. Blend, adding a little water or fruit juice if required, until you have a thick, semi-frozen smoothie. Serve at once.

Cook's Note – Griddled sliced peaches or nectarines makes a great substitute for the figs.

ACKNOWLEDGEMENTS

Being involved with *Little Tables* meant sacrificing lazy Saturday mornings sipping coffee in bed. Luckily, I had a wonderfully-talented, Saturday-sacrificing team working with me who were happy to put on their kid-friendly morning faces, despite lost coffee aromas and cosy beds. My family and husband in particular deserve multiple medals for supporting me and this three-year project (that's a lot of Saturdays). Antique shops became my second haunt while I searched for little treasures, like the perfectly-chipped teacup or vintage toy. Prop sourcing and collecting became my favourite pastime; antique dealers and shop owners knew me by name and, needless to say, I can open my own shop now. Our house became a test kitchen and, sometimes, our dinners were found in the pages of this book – the Peruvian beef casserole was a definite winner. Thank you, family, for thinking my ideas were worth the sacrifice and for your keen involvement and support.

It also really helps to have a brilliant photographer husband who understands the need to create beautiful images, so thank you, Michael, for being my cheerleader and also for your gentle guidance and input, which never overshadowed my original concept and point of view. #teamLewis

Jodie Ennik doubled up as the most over-qualified stylist and untrained kid wrangler on set. Not only did she sacrifice her Saturdays, but she also proved that a fashion stylist can be both stylish and brilliant with children, managing to get any garment on the moodiest little model. Her eye for detail is worth a tonne of gold. Thanks, Jodie, for shopping and sourcing and dressing and being my second set of eyes on shoot. Thanks also to clothing designer Thomas van Dyk for your Egyptian, Japanese, Malaysian and Vietnamese creations.

Alek Darray was the hair stylist with the biggest smile and best hot iron skills. I especially love the twins' hair! Thanks, Alek, for your patience and improvisation when working with the little ones, who can only sit still for three minutes at a time.

Every cookbook needs a food stylist, and Taryne Jakobi knew exactly which garnish to crown a dish with and which ingredient would make a good recipe substitute. I think it can be challenging to work with recipes you did not develop yourself – to make gooey rice look pretty or to style yet another pancake option – but she did a fabulous job. Thanks, Taryne, for baking and cooking after hours and for the valuable food insights and beautiful plating.

Amy was our clever researcher and writer whose love of food and words made her a dream team member. Your hours of research and genuine personal interest in the project are appreciated beyond words. I love your energy and sense of humour.

Lyn Woodward was our technical food writer who made sure the grams and millilitres added up. Thanks, Lyn, for testing and advising and for your invaluable insights and ideas that helped create these delicious recipes. I'm sure there will be a lot of kids around the world enjoying your efforts.

Anna Trapido, who wrote the foreword, is a food authority who demands respect with her qualifications and lists of awards, but I love that she has her own unique point of view and shares it in her colourful Hello Kitty dress. I've had the pleasure of working with Anna for various publications over the years. Food writer, critic and broadcaster – she has a cheffing qualification from Prue Leith Academy, an MA from the University of Cambridge and a PhD in Anthropology from the University of Witwatersrand. Her book, *To the Banqueting House*, won the gold medal at the World Gourmand Cookbook Awards in Beijing, China (2007) and her second book, *Hunger for Freedom:*

The Story of Food in the Life of Nelson Mandela, won the Special Jury Prize at the World Gourmand Cookbook Awards in Paris, France (2009). Thanks, Anna, for your kind words, for all the shoots and for sharing your milk stout oxtail recipe with me!

Kito Ribbens constructed, painted and wallpapered the sets with Pantone perfection. He can build anything after seeing a small blurry reference picture on a phone, shot from a reflective glossy magazine, and he will always answer my seventh call reminding him of some detail I had in mind. Thanks, Kito, for interpreting my briefs with your calm nature and pointing out my design flaws with a gentle correction. Nothing was too difficult or too much of a problem for you. As a dad, you also deserve a medal.

This was the second cookbook that Elena van Renen directed and designed for me; her mailbox was full of my last-minute changes, new sections and me moving text around like musical chairs. Thanks for your patience with my designer aspirations and for pulling it all together to create the perfect design for this book, even if it meant FaceTime in your PJs.

A huge thank you to all the staff at Beatnik Publishing – especially to Sally and Kitki for your enthusiasm and faith in this book. It has been an absolute pleasure to have collaborated with such a creative and fun team. I am looking forward to the next project with you guys.

And finally, without all these wonderful kids and patient mums and dads, this book would still be just an idea in my head.

THANK YOU.
You are all legends.

–Vanessa Lewis

BIBLIOGRAPHY

AUSTRALIA
Recipe Sources
http://australianfood.about.com/
http://www.bbcgoodfood.com/

CANADA
Recipe Sources
http://www.bonappetit.com/
http://www.epicurious.com/

CHINA
Recipe Sources
http://chinesefood.about.com/
http://allrecipes.com/
Recipes courtesy of Lyn Woodward

CUBA
Recipe Sources
Arroz con leche and black bean and plantain recipes
courtesy of Yummly.com

DENMARK
Recipe Sources
http://www.bonappetit.com/
http://mydanishkitchen.com/

EGYPT
Recipe Sources
http://egyptian-cuisine-recipes.com/
http://abissadacooks.blogspot.co.za/

ENGLAND
Recipe Sources
http://www.indobase.com/
http://www.italianfoodforever.com/

FRANCE
Recipe Sources
20minutecook.com/
Recipes courtesy of Lyn Woodward

GREECE
Recipe Sources
http://www.mygreekdish.com
http://www.oikosyogurt.com

ICELAND
Recipe Sources
http://icecook.blogspot.co.za/
http://rabbitfoodformybunnyteeth.com/
http://chatteringkitchen.com/

INDIA
Recipe Sources
Recipes courtesy of Lyn Woodward
http://www.food.com/
http://www.vegrecipesofindia.com/

IRELAND
Recipe Sources
http://christinascucina.com/
http://allrecipes.co.uk/

ISRAEL
Recipe Sources
http://toriavey.com/
http://www.bbc.co.uk/
http://www.simplyrecipes.com/
http://toriavey.com/

ITALY
Recipe Sources
http://www.italian-dessert-recipes.com/
http://www.foodnetwork.com/

JAMAICA
Recipe Sources
http://www.uncommoncaribbean.com/
http://www.saveur.com/
http://www.lifestylefood.com.au/

JAPAN
Recipe Sources
https://iscribbler.wordpress.com/
http://www.wikihow.com/
http://j-simplerecipes.com/
http://www.japanesecooking101.com/

JORDAN
Recipe Sources
http://arabiczeal.com/
http://www.alternativeegypt.com/

LITHUANIA
Recipe Sources
http://gbtimes.com/
http://easteuropeanfood.about.com/

MALAYSIA
Recipe Sources
http://allrecipes.com/
https://chokchow.wordpress.com/

MEXICO
Recipe Sources
http://www.foodnetwork.com/
http://www.taste.com.au/
http://www.bbcgoodfood.com/

MOROCCO
Recipe Sources
http://moroccanfood.about.com/
https://lucyinthelarder.wordpress.com/

MOZAMBIQUE
Recipe Sources
https://forgetfusion.wordpress.com/
https://easyportugueserecipes.com/

NETHERLANDS
Recipe Sources
http://dutchfood.about.com/
http://www.notquitenigella.com/

NEW ZEALAND
Recipe Sources
http://www.stuff.co.nz/
http://www.breakfast-eaters.org.nz/

PERU
Recipe Sources
http://www.quericavida.com/
http://peruvian-cuisine.blogspot.com/

PORTUGAL

Recipe Sources

http://www.epicurious.com/

Portuguese Culture Club, Pick n Pay Fresh Living Magazine, April 2013.

RUSSIA

Recipe Sources

http://natashaskitchen.com/

Various Authors, Culinaria:European Specialties

Konemann, 1995.

SCOTLAND

Recipe Sources

http://www.theguardian.com/

http://www.heraldscotland.com/

SOUTH AFRICA

Recipe Sources

https://www.ocado.com/

https://lesdachef.wordpress.com/

SWITZERLAND

Recipe Sources

http://www.saveur.com/

http://www.about.ch/

UNITED STATES OF AMERICA

Recipe Sources

Nigella Lawson, How To Be A Domestic Goddess: Baking And The Art Of Comfort Cooking.

Chatto And Windus, 2003.

http://www.thekitchn.com/

VIETNAM

Recipe Sources

http://www.foodbycountry.com/

http://www.epicurious.com/

http://www.taste.com.au/

http://vietnamcoracle.com/

CONTRIBUTORS RECIPES

Nina

Brookdale, Heavenly and Healthy Foods: Brookdale's 21 Days to a Healthy Lifestyle.

Brookdale Hydro, 2012

Vanessa

Michele Cranston, Marie Claire: 10 Years of Great Food with Michele Cranston.

Murdoch Books, 2012.

Jodie

http://www.bbcgoodfood.com/

Taryne

Dish magazine NZ

Amy

http://www.food.com/

Alek

http://ladyandpups.com/

Elena

http://www.foodnetwork.com/

Lyn

Recipes courtesy of Lyn Woodward.